Praise for *Dial 100*

'An unputdownable, high-octane thriller … a thick plot, searing narrative … a masterclass in crime storytelling.'
S. Hussain Zaidi, India's leading crime writer

'Yet another gripping book from Kulpreet Yadav, based on true-crime investigations from across the country. A must-read for those who wish to understand how the Indian police functions to outwit criminals under the most trying circumstances. A timely reminder to outlaws that they can't get away.'
Neeraj Kumar, Former Commissioner of Police, Delhi, and author of *Khaki Files*

'Justice isn't served—one must hunt for it. This book takes you on that relentless chase.'
Anup Soni, actor and host, *Crime Patrol*

'I read the stories with undivided attention, gripped as I was by the masterful narration, and felt proud of the officers who prepared the grounds for bringing the culprits to book. Kulpreet has presented yet another page-turner in his inimitable style.'
Aloke Lal, IPS, Former Director General of Police and author

'These stories showcase how real policemen, armed with the right mindset and attitude, unravel even the most complex cases. Lucidly written, highly informative and fast-paced, this book is a must-read for anyone fascinated by the art of investigation.'
Sushant Singh, actor and author

'When it comes to non-fiction—true stories of war or crime—Kulpreet Yadav has few parallels in India.'

Vish Dhamija, author of *The Mogul/Le Magnat*—winner of the Cognac Prize for Best International Novel 2024 in France

'Kulpreet's vivid storytelling in *Dial 100* makes it perfect for screen adaptation. His ability to take complex events, like the Salem train heist, and transform them into lucid, engaging narratives is truly unmatched.'

Prashant Bhagia, film director

'A gripping true-crime police procedural at its finest. Kulpreet plunges readers straight into the heart of the cases, making them feel the tension and smell the blood.'

Anirban Bhattacharyya, author of *The Deadly Dozen*, and creator and producer, *Savdhaan India*

DIAL 100

TOUGH CASES, TOUGHER POLICEMEN

KULPREET YADAV

HARPER
NON-FICTION

First published in India by Harper Non-Fiction 2025
An imprint of HarperCollins *Publishers*
HarperCollins *Publishers* India, Cyber City,
Building 10-A, Gurugram, Haryana – 122002, India
www.harpercollins.co.in

2 4 6 8 10 9 7 5 3 1

Copyright © Kulpreet Yadav 2025

P-ISBN: 978-93-6989-857-2
E-ISBN: 978-93-6989-720-9

This book is a work of non-fiction based on facts collected from a variety of sources, online and offline, and the author's interviews with people well-versed with police procedurals. The views and opinions mentioned in the book are the author's own and the facts have been verified to the extent possible. Though due care has been taken to ensure that the events related to these stories remain as true as possible, the names of the characters have been changed to justify dramatizations wherever a critical link was missing, or, a setting established to provide context. The book does not intend to hurt any sentiments or be biased in favour of, or against any particular person, society, gender, creed, nation or religion. The author and the publisher, therefore, assume no responsibility for errors, inaccuracies, omissions, or any other inconsistencies herein and disclaim any liability to any party for any loss, damage, or disruption caused by errors or omissions, whether such errors or omissions
result from negligence, accident, or any other cause.

Kulpreet Yadav asserts the moral right
to be identified as the author of this work.

All rights reserved. No part of this publication may be reproduced,
stored in a retrieval system, or transmitted, in any form or by any means,
electronic, mechanical, photocopying, recording or otherwise,
without the prior permission of the publishers.

Without limiting the exclusive rights of any author, contributor or the publisher of this publication, any unauthorized use of this publication to train generative artificial intelligence (AI) technologies is expressly prohibited. HarperCollins also exercise their rights under Article 4(3) of the Digital Single Market Directive 2019/790 and expressly reserve this publication from the text and data-mining exception.

Typeset in 11/15 Adobe Garamond Pro
by HarperCollins *Publishers* India Pvt. Ltd

Printed and bound at
Thomson Press (India) Ltd

This book is produced from independently certified FSC® paper
to ensure responsible forest management.

HarperCollins *Publishers*, Macken House, 39/40 Mayor Street Upper, Dublin 1, D01 C9W8, Ireland

This book is a tribute to the dedication of police officers who tirelessly pursue justice, often going above and beyond the call of duty. Through their efforts, they bring hope to victims, restore order to chaos and remind us of the power of integrity and perseverance in creating a safer world for everyone.

Contents

Preface — xi

CASE #1: Catch Me If You Can — 1

CASE #2: When the Rubber Meets the Road — 41

CASE #3: Back against the Wall — 61

CASE #4: Raise the Bar — 93

CASE #5: Skeleton in the Closet — 116

CASE #6: The Last Straw — 149

CASE #7: The Buck Stops Here — 179

PREFACE

The Indian police force is often stereotyped as sloppy or inefficient—a perception that, while popular, is far from the truth. The reality is more complex and challenging. With a staggering police-to-population ratio of just 150 officers per 1,00,000 citizens, India falls significantly short of the 200 mark stipulated by the United Nations. This inadequate staffing, compounded by low pay, gruelling work hours and limited opportunities for continuous training in an era of rapidly evolving technology, paints a picture of an overburdened and under-resourced force.

And yet, despite these constraints, countless police officers rise above the odds every day. They go beyond the call of duty, harnessing ingenuity, determination and cutting-edge technology—often self-taught—to solve crimes that seem impossible to crack. Their dedication, often at the expense of personal comfort and family time, deserves not just recognition but also admiration. A soldier may guard the borders of a nation, but a policeman fights wars within its boundaries, confronting invisible enemies who blend seamlessly into society. And even when criminals are apprehended, the road to conviction remains arduous, thanks to the rigorous standards of evidence and the legal complexities of our justice system.

This book, *Dial 100*, is a tribute to such unsung heroes of our society. It features seven gripping cases from recent times, each a testament to the resourcefulness, resilience and relentless pursuit of justice by the Indian police. These stories are not just about solving crimes; they are about the human element—the sleepless nights, the strategic thinking, the creative use of technology and the emotional toll borne by those who shoulder the responsibility of safeguarding our society.

As an author, I have striven to present these cases in an engaging and relatable manner, recreating dialogues and scenes to immerse readers in the pulse-pounding tension and drama of the investigations. The language is straightforward and accessible, making the book an enjoyable read for anyone curious about the inner workings of criminal investigations.

Dial 100 is my second foray into the true-crime genre, following the success of *Queens of Crime*, co-authored with actor Sushant Singh and published in 2019. The overwhelmingly positive response to that book inspired me to delve deeper into this genre and bring forth more such narratives that inform, engage and resonate with readers. I hope this book receives the same warmth and word-of-mouth appreciation as *Queens of Crime*.

There is also a secondary purpose to this work. This book serves as a cautionary tale to those who believe they can outsmart the law. No matter how sophisticated the crime, how well-planned the execution or how advanced the technology used to mask it, there will always be someone in uniform, more determined, more resourceful and more relentless, ready to bring wrongdoers to justice.

Finally, I hope that these stories inspire greater appreciation for the professionalism and commitment of the Indian police. Let us work towards building a society where the fear of justice deters criminal intent and where the law is upheld as a beacon of fairness and accountability.

Kulpreet Yadav

CASE #1
CATCH ME IF YOU CAN

Case overview and tools of investigation: Mobile tower coverage, CCTVs and a money trail from the purchase of immovable properties led to the arrest of an interstate gang from Madhya Pradesh that looted cash from a moving train in Tamil Nadu.

Location: Salem–Chennai Express route and Guna (Madhya Pradesh)

Ravi Sunderrajan took the final sip of his whisky, placed the crystal glass down and looked around. Long-legged Indian and Eastern European hostesses were serving drinks to gamblers who were busy at different tables in the casino, their eyes focused and faces flushed. Instrumental jazz played, and the air smelled of whisky, skewered meats and expensive perfume.

Over three nights, Ravi had lost all his cash. Today was his fourth night in Goa, and he stood in one corner of his favourite casino, underconfident, edgy and desperate to recover his money. However, he knew this was not possible; money lost in gambling stayed lost, unless, of course, one raised the stakes and took greater risks by putting their assets on the line.

A blonde hostess approached him with a refill.

'Sir, your single malt.' Her voice was husky yet sweet.

As she served him, Ravi winked at her, his mood lifting momentarily.

The hostess ignored him and left. It made Ravi angry, but he knew he had his rotten luck to blame for the situation he was in. He had lost six lakhs and now he had nothing. Everyone in the casino, including the hostesses, knew this.

Ravi was five feet six inches tall, a dark-complexioned man who kept his mop of black hair well oiled and combed to make sure his receding hairline stayed hidden. Every time he moved, his forehead shone and his teeth seemed whiter than his white shirt. A closet gambler, a closet womanizer and a closet thief; his family and colleagues, however, knew Ravi Sunderrajan as a family-loving, God-fearing bank clerk who lived and worked in Salem, Tamil Nadu.

His phone rang. He pressed the accept button without looking at the screen and said, 'Hello?'

Ravi almost spilled his whisky as he recognized the voice on the other end. With that, the under-confident face rearranged itself, and now he looked scared. Hurriedly, he placed his glass down and stepped out on to the deck.

Outside, the night was dark and quiet, and lights flickered at a little distance on the shore of Panjim. The floating casino was anchored in the Mandovi River.

He whispered, 'Hi, honey.'

'Hi, what took you so long to pick up the call, Ravi?'
'Oh, nothing ... I'm just tired.' He took a deep breath.
'Where are you, honey?'
'Where ... you know where I am. In Chennai, where else?'
'No, I mean, where in Chennai?'
'What happened? Is something wrong?'
'I met Joseph yesterday and he was asking about you. When I said you were in Chennai for bank work, he frowned and said that you were on leave and not on bank work.'

Ravi hesitated. Just then, a barge crossed the floating casino and sounded one long blast. The pneumatic horn was an instant giveaway.

'What sort of sound was that?'
'That?' His voice wavered. 'Oh, that's a new kind of bus, I think. Look, I'm busy, honey.'
'But ... but why did Joseph lie?'
'Okay, I didn't want to reveal this, but Joseph has left me with no choice now. The truth is that he has been told by the boss that I'm on leave so that he doesn't come to know what is happening. The bank has found that he is corrupt, and I'm investigating his case.'
'Oh ...'
'But don't tell anyone. It's top secret.'
'No, no, no, why would I tell anyone?'
'Not even your mother and sister, okay?'
'Okay.'
'I've really got to go, honey. There's a lot of paperwork to be done in Joseph's case.'

He disconnected the call, stepped back into the casino, took out his handkerchief and wiped the sweat from his forehead.

Then he gulped the whisky straight up and waved the glass as soon as his eyes met the hostess's.

The blonde hostess refilled his glass and smiled. 'Do you want to play more, Mr Ravi?'

Before he could respond, she winked at him, and Ravi was taken aback. He nodded.

She continued, 'I can introduce you to someone who can give you money to play. On credit, of course.'

He gave her a half-smile and asked, 'And how much would I owe you for this?'

'Ten thousand. Plus, you get to take me for one night and do whatever your heart desires.'

Ravi smiled from ear to ear. 'My heart desires a lot, honey. What can you do for me?'

She stepped closer and placed her hand on his leg. Then, as he started breathing rapidly, she traced a heart on his thigh with her slender fingers, her red nails shining in the dim light like moving embers. 'All your wildest dreams can come true with me.'

Ravi swallowed hard to deal with the chemical changes in his body.

After a few moments, she straightened herself, cleared her throat and whispered, 'Follow me, sir.'

Ravi followed her, his eyes on her swinging hips. They took the lift to two decks below and walked along the carpeted corridor until she stopped in front of a room. The metal plate on the door read: Meeting Room.

She turned to look at Ravi and whispered, 'My shift is till 7 a.m. See you at seven.'

Ravi nodded and stammered, 'What ... what is your name?'

She winked, emphasizing her long and artificial eyelashes. 'Valentina.'

Then, she pushed the door open for him to step inside. The door closed behind him as soon as he took a step into the room.

There were two men seated in the dimly lit room. One of them got up, took a few steps towards Ravi and extended his hand. 'Mr Ravi Sunderrajan, what a pleasure to meet you. My name is Daku Singh.'

Ravi shook his hand and sat down on one of the sofa chairs. The room had six sofa chairs, placed in a circle around a round table. The second man didn't speak or move.

'Hello, Daku Singh.'

They were quiet for a few seconds before Daku spoke again. 'Can I get you a drink?'

'Yes, er … I mean, *no*. First tell me, what are you offering?'

Daku laughed. 'In our line of business, we only offer money. If you give us what we want, we will give you hard cash.'

Ravi nodded. 'Great. I can get you a bank loan.'

'Bank loan?'

'Yes, and you can stop paying after the first EMI. I'll ensure that the bank doesn't go to the police or hire bouncers to recover the money. In fact, I will get it included in the list of bad debts. No one will come after you. Ever. For this, I would charge 20 per cent of the loan amount disbursed.'

Daku laughed harder. This time, his companion joined him too. There was something intimidating in their laughter, and red flags started popping up in Ravi's head.

Ravi had been cheating his bank for a decade now, and he had never been caught. The reason for this was his ability to see through a bluff. He had got numerous loans sanctioned that ended up as bad debts. The bank manager and, in fact, every employee at the bank knew that Ravi had something to do with the increasing number of bad debts, but they had never been able to trace any of these back to Ravi, as he never left any loose ends. The slightest doubt and he would just walk away from a prospective customer. Therefore, despite a lot of surveillance on his personal life, the bank had nothing. When in Salem, he lived a simple life and stayed away from luxuries. All the money he made through these con deals was spent in Goa and other cities to fund his addiction to gambling and sex.

On one occasion, the bank's investigation team had tailed him to Pondicherry, where he had been planning to indulge in his fantasies, but he was smart enough to spot them in time. Thereafter, for the next three days, he had only visited temples, staying there for hours and praying. Finally, he left the town and went straight home.

'Hey, where are you lost?'

Ravi got back to his senses and looked at Daku Singh, who was snapping his fingers in front of his eyes.

Ravi got up and said, 'I'm not feeling very well.'

Daku sat down heavily on the sofa he was standing next to. The two men looked at Ravi as he walked towards the door. He placed his hand on the doorknob and said, 'I'm sorry, but I need to go.'

Daku said, 'No problem.'

Then, as he opened the door and stepped out, he heard Daku say, 'In case you change your mind, we will be right here till 7 a.m.'

Ravi took the lift back to the game deck, and as soon as the doors opened, he was face to face with Valentina. She stared at him and said, 'I thought you were a man, but you turned out to be a sissy. Now go wear a skirt so that you can start attending the real men here with me—men with balls.'

He sidestepped her and walked back to his corner. As a new hostess brought him his favourite single malt, the meeting started to play in his mind again. Maybe he was overreacting; he should have at least heard what they had to offer.

Two decks below, in the meeting room, Valentina stood before Daku Singh.

Daku said, 'You got us an asshole.'

'My job was to bring him here. Thereafter, you guys had to convince him. Looks like you scared him away.'

'We were polite, sugar, and we even dressed up for the part; look at our clothes—we are dressed as gentlemen, aren't we?'

She flicked a light switch and said, 'Perhaps the room was too dark. Perhaps you guys sounded too scary. I don't know.'

The silent man switched the light off.

Daku said, 'Sugar, try one more time. Please.'

She smiled and spoke after a few moments. 'Okay, I like challenges too. He might be scared of you, umm ... *gentlemen*, but I am pretty sure he wants to get in bed with me ...'

With that, she turned and left the room.

A few seconds later, Valentina emerged from the lift and walked straight towards Ravi. Their eyes met when she was a few steps away, and he looked at her uncertainly. His confused look made her smile.

'Listen, I'm feeling very horny and I want you right now.'

'Now? But I don't have money. You know that, don't you?'

'I don't want your *money*. I just want *you*.'

With that, she turned, and this time, Ravi's mind completely stopped working as he followed her, his eyes glued to her swinging hips again.

One deck below, moments later, Valentina opened room 203, and Ravi grabbed her as soon as the door closed. Both fell on to the bed. It was passionate lovemaking, one that gave way to more sessions over the next few hours, alternatingly tender and rough. Finally, Ravi lit a cigarette and whispered, 'Thank you.'

'Hmm …'

After a few minutes, Valentina placed her head on Ravi's chest and said, 'We can do this more often if you want. In fact, we can go somewhere on a trip together. You know, like lovers.'

Ravi inhaled deeply and said, 'I'm just a clerk in a bank, Valentina. You know that I have no money.'

'You don't need money to do what your heart desires, honey. You need a smart mind, and I am sure your head is as fertile as that tool between your legs.'

Ravi laughed. 'Hey, that's vulgar, Valentina.'

'Vulgar? You are lying naked in the arms of an escort in a casino after losing all your money and are greedy to get more somehow, while your wife waits for you at home, and you call my words vulgar? Really?'

He looked at her. She seemed dead serious, and Ravi's heart sank a little. Was he doing the right thing? The next second, she laughed, and he knew the answer—of course, he was doing the right thing, because the excitement of all this was blowing his mind.

He extinguished his cigarette and placed another one between his lips. She took the lighter from the side table and lit it. Ravi inhaled and asked, 'Okay, tell me, how do I use my mind to make more money so that I can play?'

'Now we are getting somewhere. Let me put it this way. The right mind has the ability to spot the right information, and information is money.'

'Hmm ... but what kind of information can a bank clerk have?' He stopped speaking and sat down suddenly as something dawned on him. 'The men you had taken me to—are they information buyers?'

'Spot on, and they will give you a lot of money for the right information.'

'Hmm ...'

'Look, proving who sold the information is nearly impossible in a court of law. On the other hand, committing a crime based on the information is dangerous, and it is always the criminals who are caught or killed during the crime, and many are convicted. The information sellers get away every time.'

When Ravi didn't say anything, and Valentina knew she had plunged her knife deep into him, she continued, 'The men you met today are seeking information. If you give them something they can use, they will give you a lot of money upfront.'

Ravi frowned. 'But what's in it for you?'

'Well, if you are willing to have a proper meeting with them and not run away like you did the last time, I will get my money from them. Ten thousand. Which I think is fair, because now that you have used me, you owe me ten thousand too, you naughty boy.'

'So you earn twenty thousand in one night, right?'

She winked in response as Ravi got up and got dressed. He suddenly felt clearheaded. But before he could decide what to do next, he had one final question. 'What if they are the police or investigating officers from my bank's head office?'

She smiled and replied, 'I have been working with them for the last five years, honey. They are hardcore criminals, as criminal as they come.'

By now, Ravi had put on his clothes. He smiled. 'So we are meeting for that 7 a.m. treat, aren't we?'

She laughed and threw a pillow at him. 'Get out. They are waiting.'

Ravi laughed and left.

Daku Singh opened the door when Ravi knocked. Everything was the same as earlier, the only difference this time around being Ravi's mood—he was now smiling from ear to ear. Instead of shaking Daku's hand, he slapped his back as if they were close friends before walking into the room.

Daku Singh pulled his extended hand back and followed Ravi in. The silent man stayed silent, but Ravi waved to him. The man waved back.

Daku cleared his throat. 'Valentina's magic never fails to work. Everyone wants to talk after she has fucked them.'

The thought of Valentina fucking other men diluted some of Ravi's enthusiasm, but he continued to smile.

Daku took a deep breath and said, 'We know everything about you, so you don't have to introduce yourself. But we need to tell you who we are before we start.'

'You know everything about me?'

Daku raised his hand to reduce the alarm in Ravi's voice. 'I mean, we know where you work and that you have no police record. And that you love gambling and try out different women. It's cool—there's nothing wrong 'with that'? Ninety per cent of men are exactly like you, us included. The only difference between others and you, however, is that you are a lot smarter than them. Right so far?'

'Maybe ... now tell me, who are you?'

'We are thieves. That's the long and short of it. We live in Madhya Pradesh, but we travel all over the country to steal. We have been caught a few times, but we are clean now, out in the open, looking for a big hit.'

'Okay ... what do you steal and how can I help you do that? Also, you said I'm smarter than the others. How?'

'Okay, I say you are smarter than the others because you have not been caught, though you have been cheating your bank for a long time now! Look, what we need from you is nothing difficult or big. In fact, it will be easier than the easiest bank loan you have got sanctioned for one of your clients.'

They were quiet for a minute before Ravi asked, 'I know you want information. But what kind of information can I trade with you?'

'Good question. What we want to know is your bank's cash transfer schedule from Salem to Chennai for the RBI.'

'You mean the train name and dates, etc.?'

'Yes.'

'That's all?'

'That's all.'

Ravi scratched his chin. 'And what do you intend to do with this information? I'm asking because the train leaves heavily guarded with a dozen-plus policemen who have automatic weapons. The seal of the parcel van in which the money is carried is inspected at every station where the train stops. So if you are planning to rob the train, I must tell you right now that it is next to impossible.'

'Well, what we do with that information is our problem. We will pay you twenty lakhs for this. Half now and half later.'

'Now?'

'Of course. You have two more days here in Goa, don't you? Fuck Valentina as many times as you want and play high-stakes games at the VIP tables in the casino. Who knows, you might leave this place with a lot of money …'

Ravi was finding it hard to believe. 'I'm sorry, but I don't see any value in this information because, as I said, you can't rob the bank's money. So what will you do with this information? Come on. Before I say yes, I want to know. Otherwise, I might die of curiosity before I pass on the information to you.'

The silent man smiled and spoke for the first time. 'You have a good sense of humour, Ravi, but your questions aren't too smart. I would expect someone like you to know when to stop asking questions.'

Ravi frowned and looked at him. 'And what is your name?'

'I'm Daku Singh's brother. My name is Kallu Singh.'

'So is it a yes?' Daku asked.

Ravi nodded, took a deep breath and said, 'Yes. So where is my advance of ten lakhs.'

Daku pulled out a bag from under his sofa chair and placed it on the centre table. Then, his eyes on Ravi, he unzipped it and said, 'Here.'

Ravi bent forward and his eyes widened in shock at what he saw. The bag had pistols, ammunition magazines and short-barrelled automatic rifles.

Seeing Ravi's reaction, Daku Singh looked down with a menacing smile. 'Sorry, wrong bag.'

He closed the bag and pushed it back under the sofa. Then he pulled out another bag, opened it to check and smiled. 'It's all here.'

This time, Ravi bent forward a lot slower, his eyes on the two brothers. Then he flicked his head down for a second to check. The money was there.

Ravi picked up the bag and walked out of the room, his heart beating wildly. Once on the main deck, he looked at the clock on the wall. It was 7 a.m. Just then, he felt a delicate hand reach for his waist from behind. He turned and saw Valentina there, pouting at him. She had changed from her hostess's uniform into a two-piece bikini.

'Now that you have this bag, would you want my services this morning too, my master?'

Ravi grabbed her and they walked out together.

Two days later, having lost almost all the money that Daku and Kallu had given him, Ravi bid farewell to Valentina and left Goa with a heavy heart. He didn't want this holiday, where he was spending his days in the arms of Valentina and nights at the gambling tables, to end.

Finally, when he reached his home in Salem, he had only twenty thousand rupees left with him. For the next two days, totally exhausted, all Ravi did was sleep. His wife was relieved that her husband was finally back after finishing his investigation related to Joseph. As promised, she had not discussed it with anyone, not even with her mother and sister. Now every time she saw Julie, Joseph's wife, she felt pity for the poor woman, as her husband was about to be taken away by the police.

Three days later, at the breakfast table, Ravi gulped down the idlis made by his wife and remarked, 'Darling, I missed you. No one in Chennai can make idlis half as good as you.'

She blushed and replied, 'Thank you. Can I say something that has been bothering me for the last few days, honey?'

Alarmed, Ravi looked up sharply. 'Yes?'

'I know I shouldn't poke my nose into your office affairs, but if possible, please be kind to Joseph when the policemen come to ask you questions based on your investigation.'

'Oh!' So much had happened after the phone call from his wife when he was in Goa that it took him a few seconds to recognize his own lie.

She continued, 'Please, he is not such a bad man. We have known them for the past ten years, and Julie is so close to me. She will be devastated, poor woman.'

Ravi inhaled deeply and said, 'Don't worry. I have already taken care of it, honey. Maybe the police won't come after all because all the evidence that was given to me seemed fabricated or inconclusive. I have recommended that no action should be taken.'

'Really? Wow! You are so kind, honey.'

A week later, on 1 August 2016, Ravi called Daku Singh from a local shop in Salem town. 'Hello, is this Daku Singh?'

'Yes.'

'This is Ravi. The information is ready.'

'Tell me.'

'Okay, the International Overseas Bank has booked a cargo van on the Salem–Chennai Express that will depart on 8 August 2016. The currency is old but usable, and I'm not sure of the exact amount, but it will be around 300 crores. The money is in Rs 500 and Rs 1000 denominations, stored in two hundred or so wooden boxes. The recipient is the Reserve Bank of India in Chennai.'

'Thank you.'

'How do I get my balance money?'

'You want the cash in Salem or in Goa?'

Ravi thought for a couple of seconds before replying, 'I want it in Goa next month.'

'Consider it done.' The call was disconnected.

Ravi placed the phone down. He had kept his voice low and had called after making sure that the shopkeeper was attending to a customer on the other side of the shop and had not heard him. Then he walked away quickly so that the shopkeeper wouldn't remember his face.

The shop was not far from the bank, and Ravi was back in his chair within five minutes, his face lit and his smile wider than usual.

⚭

Daku Singh and Kallu Singh arrived in Chinnasalem, a small taluk in Tamil Nadu, in the early hours of 6 August. They had left Guna in Madhya Pradesh in a Tata Safari along with three other members of their gang, covering the distance of 1,863 kilometres along the Srinagar–Kanyakumari Highway (NH 44) in a little under two days.

Before getting out of the vehicle, Daku turned and spoke in a firm voice. 'No one will leave their rooms. This is a very small town of just twenty thousand people. We can't blend in, so no talking to the locals. We will leave for the railway station after 10 p.m. Until then, take rest. Okay?'

The five of them got out and checked into a cheap lodge using fake IDs. They booked two rooms, one for the brothers and the second one for the remaining three.

Daku and Kallu had long hair now, and they wore caps with grease marks on them. The idea was to look like poor Bihari workers, and they looked the part. Had Ravi passed them on the street, he wouldn't have recognized the brothers. Their assistants wore no caps as they were new members of the gang who had no criminal records anywhere and were not likely to be recognized. Daku and Kallu had been arrested a few times before and had to be sure their getup was good enough to evade suspicion.

In the afternoon, Daku walked across the road from the lodge and got five packets of biryani and Coca-Colas for everyone. The gang members were given the food in their rooms.

At 10.30 p.m., the five of them left for the Chinnasalem railway station.

The gang members had been briefed about the mission and their roles in detail in Guna before departing, but Daku Singh repeated it. 'Today is the sixth of August. It's our rehearsal day.

The actual mission will take place on the eighth, that is, the day after tomorrow. The Salem–Chennai express departs from Salem at 9.40 p.m. every night. Chinnasalem is around 87 kilometres from Salem. On the eighth, you will drop Kallu and me with our gas cutter at the station at 10 p.m. Then, you take the Safari and start driving towards Vriddhachalam station. While you are on your way, the Salem–Chennai express will arrive at Chinnasalem at 11.09 p.m. That's the scheduled time of arrival. We will be ready on the non-platform side by then, and as soon as the train stops, we will climb on to the roof. The train will stop for one minute only. That's only sixty seconds, so we will be quick. This, as you know, is the most difficult part of the mission, but since it will be late at night, most people will be asleep. Once we are on the roof, we will wait for the train to leave the station. After that, we will get to work. By then, the three of you will have reached halfway to Vriddhachalam station along NH 79. The scheduled time of arrival at Vriddhachalam station is 12.10 a.m. The train will halt there for ten minutes because the diesel engine will be removed and an electric engine will be put in its place. Ten minutes is enough for us to get down and escape. Before we jump off, we will have thrown the bags full of money to the two of you a hundred metres before the station after spotting your torch signal. Clear so far?'

Everyone nodded, the street lamps and the lights from roadside shops intermittently illuminating and shadowing their faces as the vehicle moved.

Daku Singh continued, 'While you are waiting outside in the Safari, keep adjusting the position so that there are no vehicles ahead blocking our way and we can leave immediately after we reach. In today's rehearsal, Kallu and I will observe the train and you will wait right outside the station. Once we are back, we will return to the lodge. Okay?'

Everyone nodded again.

By midnight, they were back at the lodge. The recce had been successful. No one had boarded the train at Chinnasalem, and just two passengers had alighted. The platform on which the train had stopped was deserted. Since it was late at night, there were no food vendors either. Daku and Kallu had picked a dark spot on the opposite platform. They were the only ones there. As soon as the train had stopped, the two of them had jumped on to the tracks and approached the train from its non-platform side. They had then paused next to the train, looking left and right. Still no one. All they had to do now was climb up. The train had started to move just then, and they quickly turned back and climbed onto the opposite platform. A few minutes later, they were back in the waiting car.

In the lodge now, all of them had gathered in Daku and Kallu's room. They had picked up a bottle of cheap rum on the way and bought another five packets of biryani. Within minutes, they were drinking and eating.

Kallu spoke this time. 'Okay, guys, listen to me. This should be a cakewalk. In less than two days, we will all be on our way home richer by a few crores.'

Daku raised his glass. 'Tomorrow, we will rest. And no alcohol after this until we are safely out of the reach of the police.'

'Cheers!' It was Kallu this time.

All raised their plastic glasses and said in chorus: 'Cheers!'

One of the highlights of the mission was not to try to loot all the money but only a few crores. According to the information given by Ravi, the scheduled arrival of the train at Chennai Egmore railway station was at 3.50 a.m., and the RBI officials were only expected to arrive for the collection of the sealed boxes of cash by 9 a.m. Until then, the train would be in the loco shed under the protection of armed guards belonging to the Tamil Nadu police. This meant that the robbery would be discovered nine hours after the gang had departed the Vriddhachalam station. By then, they would have crossed two state borders, and since not a soul knew where they were from—not even Ravi—no one would ever come looking for them.

On 8 August 2016, everything started like clockwork. Before the arrival of the train, Daku Singh and Kallu Singh were on the opposite platform at the Chinnasalem station, standing in the darkest spot with their caps lowered to avoid being detected by anyone. They already knew that there were no cameras on the platform but were not taking any chances.

The brothers had one bag each strapped to their backs. While one bag had a gas-cutting machine that they had bought from a shipyard in Goa, the other one had eight large bags folded neatly. They also had a ten-kilogram gas cylinder that had been painted black, and they were holding it between themselves with one hand each.

As scheduled, the Salem–Chennai express pulled into the station at 11.09 p.m.

As soon as the train stopped, Daku and Kallu jumped onto the tracks, trying to look as casual as possible. But the clock was ticking in their minds. Within thirty seconds, they reached the spot next to the train where they thought the risk was minimal.

Then, glancing left and right, the two of them climbed a pole and descended onto top of the train along with their bags and the cylinder. Here, they lay flat on their stomachs, the handles of their bags hooked onto their wrists and the cylinder sandwiched between their bodies. So far, so good.

The train started to move at 11.10 p.m. As soon as the train was fully swallowed by the dark night and the city's lights were behind them, the two brothers sat down cross-legged and looked at each other. They exchanged a smile. The August night air felt pleasant on their faces. It was time to start the work.

In his third and final call an hour ago, Ravi had informed Daku of the exact location of the parcel van in which the money was stored. He had also informed them that some of the money was kept in an adjacent compartment, where a few of the armed personnel would be guarding it. But the parcel van would be sealed with no one inside, he had assured them.

It took the brothers half an hour to cut a square hole of two feet by two feet on top of the parcel compartment using the gas cutter. Then, using a rope that Kallu held on the roof of the train, Daku lowered himself into the compartment. It was pitch dark. He could smell wood. His heart racing, Daku took out his torch and checked his surroundings. Indeed, he was surrounded by more than two hundred wooden boxes full of money.

On the rooftop, Kallu called his gang members. 'Is everything okay?'

'Yes, boss. How are things at your end?'

'All is well. See you at ten minutes past midnight.'

Inside the compartment, Daku was shoving the iron rod into the locks and breaking them one by one.

After he had opened around ten boxes, he shouted, 'Kallu, throw me the bags.'

He got no response. A shadow of worry crossed his face. He took out his phone and called Kallu.

'Kallu, where are you?'

'Right here, brother.'

'Throw me the bags.'

'Yes.'

He threw eight large bags into the van. One by one, Daku filled them and tied them to the rope for Kallu to pull them all the way up. That way, within minutes, they had eight bags full of Rs 500 and Rs 1,000 notes resting on top of the train.

The brothers now had around ten minutes before the train reached Vriddhachalam station. Daku called his wife back in Guna. He was feeling euphoric about what they had accomplished.

'Hey, darling, how are you?'

'I'm good, Daku. Where are you? You sound very happy.'

'Yes, I'm in Bhopal. A good business deal has come through. I will be home in two days.'

'Very good. What is that noise in the background? It sounds like a train.'

'Yes, I'm sitting at a place close to the railway tracks. I have to go now. See you soon.'

He disconnected and looked at Kallu. Kallu called his wife too. As soon as he hung up, they could see the Vriddhachalam station at a little distance. The train slowed down, and around a hundred metres short of the station, they spotted two of their gang members waiting for them. The brothers threw the cash bags to them.

Minutes later, as the train came to a halt at the station, they lowered themselves onto the non-platform side with the cylinder and the bag in which they had the gas-cutting machine. Seconds later, they were walking away from the train. The exit was simple. There were no guards, and they soon spotted their Safari.

As soon as they got in, the driver turned to check and then started driving. A few minutes later, they picked up the two men with the money bags and started to move northwards on the Kanyakumari–Srinagar Highway. All of them knew they were safe for the next nine hours and should now put as much distance between themselves and the train as possible. The SUV cut through the night in top gear.

The heist was successful. The gang had enough food in the vehicle to last them until Guna. As soon as the vehicle was safely on the highway, Daku Singh was the first to shout.

'We're rich, guys. Well done!'

Everyone shouted, 'We're rich! We're rich!'

Back at Vriddhachalam station, two police guards got down and approached the parcel van in which the cash was stored. On their way, they passed a few vendors selling tea and snacks. One of the guards was carrying a register in his hand, and both had 9 mm carbines dangling from their shoulders.

When they reached the parcel van, they stopped and checked the lock.

One of them said, 'The seal is intact.'

The other one looked at him, frowned and said, 'What did you expect?'

He laughed and said, 'I expected the seal to be intact, and it *is* intact.'

'Enter it in the register quickly and let's go and get some tea. I'm already feeling sleepy.'

The other guard opened the register and entered the 'all-okay' report.

Then the two of them rushed to the closest tea vendor and bought two cups of tea. After this, while one of them entered the compartment holding both cups of tea, the other walked to the second AC compartment and saluted the Assistant Commissioner of Police (ACP). 'Sir, all is okay.'

The ACP, who was the overall incharge of the movement of cash, looked at him and said, 'Thank you.'

The guard rushed back to his compartment and took his cup of tea as the train started to move.

As the train continued its movement towards Chennai, the guards got down at every railway station the train halted at and physically inspected the sealed lock on the parcel van. In total, ten such inspections of the seal were carried out at the ten stations where the train stopped before it arrived at the Chennai Egmore railway station.

Everything was routine, and the police were sure that no one in the world could succeed in stealing the nation's money, even if they tried. Their security had not failed even once and, therefore, they had no reason to doubt anything. The guards snacked whenever they found food at the stations and sipped tea, walking up and down to check the seal they knew would very much be there. It was boring, but they were used to this boring routine.

Finally, at 3.50 a.m. on 9 August 2016, the train arrived at Chennai Egmore station and the passengers started to deboard. Fifteen minutes later, the empty train moved to the loco shed for cleaning and inspection before the return journey. The ACP and the dozen guards were the only people on the train.

Once it reached the loco shed, the ACP addressed all the guards. 'Our mission is not over yet. The visits to check the seal on the parcel van must continue every hour, okay?'

The guards nodded, and the inspections continued.

At nine that morning, when the RBI staff didn't turn up as promised, the ACP called the mobile number that had been given to him.

'We are at Egmore, saar, but the RBI staff have not arrived.'

The voice on the other end said, 'There's a delay. They will be there in half an hour.'

'Okay, saar.'

Finally, the RBI staff arrived at 10 a.m. There was just one person from the RBI, accompanied by four armed constables from the Tamil Nadu police.

He declared on arrival, 'My apologies. I was caught up with something important.'

The ACP didn't respond and instead turned towards his guards and ordered, 'Open the seal in front of saar.'

One of the guards, suppressing a yawn, opened the lock. The RBI officer was the first to step inside. His jaw dropped. A few boxes were open and some of the currency bundles were scattered on the floor.

He shouted, 'What the hell! Hey, come here!'

The ACP went inside first, followed by the guards. There was a beam of sunlight entering the van from above. As all of them looked up, they discovered a two-foot-by-two-foot hole in the roof.

'But how is this possible?' murmured the ACP.

'What do you mean, how is it possible? Take a good look. That's the hole in your career. Be ready to pay the price for your sloppiness.'

The ACP turned sharply to look at his guards, who raised their eyebrows in equal surprise. 'You fools, how did this happen?'

The guards looked at the hole and the ACP. They had no answer.

The RBI officer was on the phone immediately, 'Saar, the money from the Salem-Chennai express has been looted.'

He listened for a while and then said, 'No, saar, the guards are here. There is a hole in the compartment's roof.'

The ACP and the guards were not allowed to leave. The compartment was sealed once again and the wait began for a proper crime scene investigation by officers of the Tamil Nadu police.

By evening that day, over a dozen police officers had arrived at the scene, including senior officers from the police headquarters in Chennai. The money had been counted and it was discovered that Rs 5 crores and 75 lakhs were short out of the total amount of 342 crores that had been stored in 226 wooden boxes.

The story of the train robbery hit the TV news by noon, and all sorts of theories started to float around. One channel called it the biggest-ever train robbery in the history of India. Another compared it to great train robberies in other countries. Yet another said it could be connected to Pakistani terrorists and now the city of Chennai was under grave threat. By sunset, the TV crew were interviewing rickshaw pullers, ragpickers and fruit sellers from around Egmore railway station. The news caught the airwaves like never before.

The Director General of Police (DGP) knew the implications of this big case. This had to be solved. A proactive approach was the need of the hour.

As a first step, he called the Inspector General (IG) of the western zone of the Tamil Nadu police, under whose jurisdiction the Salem area was located.

'Prem Kumar, saw the news?'

'Yes, sir.'

'What do you think?'

'Sir, this has been done somewhere between Salem and Vriddhachalam stations.'

'Why so?'

'Because after Vriddhachalam, the diesel engine is replaced with the electric engine. The rest of the route is electrified. Getting on the roof would be impossible after that.'

'Okay. So what's your plan of action?'

'Sir, I have already had a word with the IG of Salem town. We are moving on this as fast as we can.'

'Thank you.' The DGP hung up.

In Salem, Inspector General Prem Kumar was staring at the map of Salem District on his wall as he put the phone down.

CASE #1: CATCH ME IF YOU CAN

Then, slowly, his eyes still on the map, he got up and walked towards it. He was concentrating on the train route from Salem to Vriddhachalam.

Five minutes later, he called his assistant. 'I want a meeting with all the senior officers of my range at 7 p.m.'

The news of the robbery reached Ravi's bank by that afternoon. The staff stopped working and the volume of the TV was raised. The bank employees were wide-eyed, and even the customers' eyes were glued to the TV. All work had stopped.

Ravi was the only one who knew what was coming. But like everyone else, he too stared at the TV screen, his eyes wide. Next to him stood Joseph.

'What the fuck, man!' Joseph said, looking at Ravi.

'Yes, what the fuck, man,' replied Ravi.

'I mean, who could do such a thing? But more importantly, who leaked this information about the movement of the money?'

'I think someone from the railways. Those bastards are really corrupt.'

Joseph nodded. 'Or the police. Those bastards are more corrupt.'

'Maybe.'

'Someone from the bank could have also done it, don't you think?'

'It's possible but highly unlikely.'

'Why?'

'Because bank guys are nice.'

'I agree.'

That evening, Ravi's wife had prepared his favourite curry and rice for dinner. But he was not hungry.

She asked him, 'What's wrong, honey? Why are you not eating?'

'What's wrong? Don't you know?'

'I know about the robbery. But what's your fault?'

Ravi's thoughts turned towards Goa, where ten lakh rupees and Valentina were waiting for him. Those guys were smart, he thought. With that, some of his hunger returned and he looked at his wife. 'You are right. Let's eat.'

On the evening of 10 August 2016, Daku Singh, Kallu Singh and their three accomplices got out of the Safari near a small house located at the end of an unlit street. They were in the suburbs of Guna, a town in Madhya Pradesh with a population of less than two lakh.

It was dusk, and there were no houses in the vicinity. All they could hear were the songs of the birds ending the day and flying towards the west in flocks.

They stretched and smiled at one another. Although the nonstop journey had tired their bodies, there was a spark in their eyes.

Daku opened the gate of the house and said, 'This house belongs to my cousin. He will not disturb us. Welcome!'

Kallu and the other three picked up the bags full of money and brought them inside. Once the money bags and their luggage were safely inside, they closed the gate. It was a spacious house with a large courtyard and four rooms on one side. The courtyard had high walls around it with barbed wire on top.

After they sat down on the charpoys in the courtyard, Daku said, 'What do you guys want first, party or money?'

The accomplices looked at one another and laughed. Then one of them said, 'Sir, both.'

It was Daku's turn to laugh. He looked at Kallu and nodded.

Kallu got up, opened the courtyard's gate and stepped out. One of the accomplices closed the gate as they heard the sound of the Safari starting up and moving away.

Another one asked, 'Brother Daku, if your cousin who owns this house comes now and asks us about the money, what will we tell him?'

'He cannot come here anymore.'

'I don't understand.'

Daku's voice was cold. 'Kallu and I killed him before leaving for Salem.'

All three of them were sitting on one charpoy. They looked at him, their jaws dropping.

Daku pointed to the charpoy. 'His body is four feet under your cot.'

There was silence for one full minute. Then one of them said, 'Daku brother, we can party some other time. Right now, please give us our share so that we can go away.'

Daku laughed. 'What are you saying? You deserve a party. Have patience. Kallu will be back soon with booze and women.'

They looked at one another helplessly as Daku started to sing a song.

For the next hour, Daku sang and the others just listened. Finally, they heard the sound of an approaching vehicle. Then there was a knock on the gate. They could hear the sound of women talking.

Daku opened the gate and in walked four sex workers, followed by Kallu.

For the whole night, they drank and spent time with the women. Finally, after Kallu dropped them off and returned, Daku summoned everyone to the courtyard again.

'Okay, the party is over, boys, so let's talk business. We have decided to pay you ten lakhs each. You take the money and disappear. Spend it wisely. If anything comes back to me or Kallu, we will not only kill you but also wipe out your entire family. That's a promise.'

The men nodded as Kallu gave them their money and left the house.

In Salem, Ravi was a nervous wreck. He was reading every word about the robbery in the newspaper at his house and the three newspapers to which the bank subscribed, besides following the news on the radio and TV. During breaks, he also eavesdropped on groups of bank employees when they talked among themselves.

But it was not enough and, therefore, to ease his nervousness, he started to visit a bar on his way back from the bank every day. What began as a few pegs of whisky slowly started to consume his sanity as he drank more and more. His wife watched him silently and thought it was perhaps the pressure of work at the bank.

One night, desperate and confused, he called Valentina in Goa from the bar.

'Hello, Valentina, it's Ravi.'

'Ravi who?'

'Ravi from Salem. We met—'

'Hey, mister, my name is Maria and I don't know any Valentina. If you call again, I will give your number to the police.'

The phone almost dropped from Ravi's hand. He decided never to call her again.

In Chennai, two weeks after the robbery, when the police could not find a single lead, the DGP was summoned to the chief minister's office.

'What is happening, DGP?' the chief minister asked.

'Madam, we are doing all that we can. It's a perfect heist, totally unprecedented. But every possible lead is being pursued.'

'I want results.'

'Madam, the time has come to transfer the case to the CB-CID.'

'Do whatever you want, but this is shameful. How can someone steal so much money right from under our noses and we're left with no clue?'

'Yes, madam.'

He saluted and left.

Later that day, Anil Raaj, a DIG in the Crime Branch of the CID, was given charge of the case, and the first thing he did was form his team. It comprised one SP named Rajesh Kumar, one DSP named Javed Ali, one inspector named Sukumaran T. and one head constable named Senthil Kumar.

At 8 p.m. on the same day, the team met at the Police Research Centre (PRC) located at the CB-CID headquarters in Guindy, central Chennai.

Anil Raaj began. 'Okay, welcome, guys. We know each other, so let's skip the introductions.'

He was standing right next to a map of Tamil Nadu that hung from the wall. The others were seated.

Anil Raaj continued, 'This is an important mission, as you already know. It might be one of the most important missions of our careers. This train robbery has become such an embarrassment for the police force.'

He paused and looked at the faces of his team members before continuing, 'It's the railway police's fault. That's a fact. But it is also a fact that the state police has failed to locate the gangsters involved in this. The chief minister is breathing down the DGP's neck and the robbery has become national news.' He took a deep breath and said, 'And now this seemingly impossible-to-crack case has landed in our laps. We can either see this as a burden that will eventually stain our careers, or'—he paused for effect—'we can see this as an opportunity. Rajesh, you go first; where do you propose we start?'

'Thank you, sir, and greetings, friends. I see this as an opportunity. I know all our efforts have failed so far, but let's think out of the box.'

Anil nodded and looked at Javed.

Javed began, 'Sir, I think human intelligence is failing here. We must make use of technology.'

Sukumaran cleared his throat. 'Sir, I have been with the cyber cell for four years now. I think we can start from there. Senthil has been with me for two years, and we can use all our resources and see if the thieves have left a trail.'

Anil nodded. 'I agree. In today's day and age, there has to be some digital trace of the thieves. This has not been done by one or two men but a whole team. They must have carried out reconnaissance, surely a few dry runs, and must have had someone from the bank or the railways helping them. That's a lot of activity done by a lot of people, and I agree with Sukumaran— there has to be a trace.'

Rajesh said, 'You are right, sir. But I feel we should do some legwork too.'

Anil nodded and summed up the meeting: 'Sukumaran and Senthil, you stick to cyber investigation and report directly to me, and you, Rajesh and Javed, use the traditional investigative methods. We will meet every day at 9 a.m. to review the progress and to decide what we should do next. Clear?'

They all replied, 'Yes, sir.'

In Guna, after their accomplices had left, Daku looked at Kallu and said, 'It's time we leave this house with all the money.'

Kallu nodded.

Thereafter, Daku and Kallu picked up the bags and placed them in the Safari. From Guna city, they drove straight to their village.

On arrival, Kallu asked Daku, 'Where should we hide the money, brother?'

'Easy, Kallu. Let's keep the money bags in the room where hay is stored for the buffaloes.'

'Good idea.'

For the next month, they didn't spend any money and silently followed the news about the train robbery in Tamil Nadu. They had disposed of their SIM cards on their way to Guna, and there was no way anyone could connect them to the robbery.

Once the news died down, the brothers decided to put their money to good use. Over the next two months, Daku and Kallu bought several properties, both agricultural and commercial, in their names and in the names of their wives and children.

By November 2016, they were left with only two crores. But before they could buy their next property, something unexpected was about to happen that would render all the remaining money useless.

Here is how this disaster unfolded.

On 8 November 2016, while Daku was drinking whisky in the house, his brother, Kallu, visited him.

'What's wrong, Kallu? Why are you looking so worked up?'

'Brother, we have a big problem.'

'Problem? What happened?'

'I just heard on the TV that our prime minster has announced demonetization.'

'Demonetization? What the hell is that?'

'It means that our notes that are hidden under the hay are now less valuable than the hay itself.'

'Oh my God! This means our notes are now just paper?'

'Yes, brother.'

It was a major setback for Daku and Kallu, but they could do nothing except curse their fate.

In Chennai, the CB-CID team, under the leadership of Anil Raaj, was doing everything they could. They rounded up thousands of people and interrogated them; they used every scrap of information they got and sent their team hunting; they went through CCTV footage, tried running fingerprints they had gathered from parts of the train and the bank, announced a reward for credible information and visited red-light areas and liquor dens the thieves could have visited after stealing the money, but all their efforts came to naught.

In the cyber cell too, despite best efforts, there were no leads. The PRC had a good library with many case studies and books. Considerable time was spent by the team there too, studying cases that were similar to the train robbery.

One of the major problems for the investigative team was the fact that the stolen notes were all used and no record of their serial numbers was available. The money was, therefore, impossible to trace.

Over the next two years, Anil Raaj and his team did everything they could, but they didn't get a breakthrough, and all their time, effort and the state's money went to waste. Even in the face of failure, the only right thing the team did was that they didn't stop looking.

Then one day, they spotted a ray of hope.

Senthil visited Sukumaran and said, 'Sir, I have discovered something unusual.'

Sukumaran looked up from his laptop and said, 'Go on.'

'Sir, when the train was moving from Chinnasalem to Vriddhachalam, several calls were made to one particular village in the Guna district of Madhya Pradesh.'

'That's not unusual, Senthil. They could have been made by a few labourers.

'Could have been, but they were not.'

'What do you mean?'

'Two numbers were in the train and three were on the road that goes from Chinnasalem railway station to Vriddhachalam railway station. All five made calls to one another and to the same village in Guna. Up to here, it seems normal, but there's more.'

Sukumaran's eyes had lit up by now. He spoke with a childlike urgency. 'Go on, Senthil.'

'All five numbers went off the grid around the same time that night. The last known location was somewhere along the Srinagar–Kanyakumari Highway.'

He beamed. 'I think we have got the guys. Have you found out the addresses?'

Senthil smiled widely and said, 'Yes, sir.'

Sukumaran was soon on the phone with Anil Raaj.

The next morning, Anil Raaj, Sukumaran and Senthil were on their way. They took the flight to Bhopal, and on landing at two in the afternoon, along with two inspectors of the Madhya Pradesh police who were waiting for them, they started to move northwards towards Guna in two jeeps.

Meanwhile, in his village, Daku's new number rang. He picked it up and said, 'Harish, how are you?'

Harish, a constable in the Madhya Pradesh police who was calling from Guna, said, 'Daku, the Chennai police is here and they are on their way to arrest you. You have two hours.'

Daku disconnected the call and called Kallu and the other accomplices. He simultaneously asked his wife to pack. After this, Daku and Kallu pulled out the money bags from under the haystack and burned them.

The temperature started to dip around sunset, as Anil Raaj and his team, accompanied by the policemen from the Madhya Pradesh police, arrived in the village to raid the addresses Senthil had found out from the telephone company.

To the horror of Anil Raaj and the others, the thieves had learnt of the raid and left minutes before their arrival. The ash from the notes was still hot. Clearly, there was a mole in the Madhya Pradesh police.

They spoke to the neighbours, and it didn't take long for Anil Raaj to find out that the brothers had bought a few properties during the last two years. On his way back to Bhopal, he called the DGP, Tamil Nadu police. 'Sir, someone tipped off the thieves and they took off before we arrived. But the MP police is on the hunt and their properties are being seized. They will be smoked out of the hole they are hiding in soon.'

'Good job, Anil. We will do a press conference once these guys are arrested and brought to Chennai.'

'Yes, sir.'

'Any idea who their contact was in the railway or the Salem bank?'

'Not at the moment, sir. But once we arrest the thieves, I'm sure they will start singing.'

'I agree. So who from your team cracked this?'

'Senthil, sir. He's a head constable in our cyber cell.'

'Fantastic! Do recommend his name for an award, okay?'

'Sure, sir.'

While the Tamil Nadu and Madhya Pradesh police teams were conducting the raid in Guna, Ravi Sunderrajan landed in Goa. Since the police operation was being conducted discreetly, as far as he was concerned, two years was a long time and the case had turned cold.

For the last year, there had not been a single news report about the Salem train robbery case anywhere. Therefore, his nerves eased, Ravi had given in to his urge to gamble and told his wife that he had to go to Chennai for a few days.

She had said only one word—'Joseph?'—and he had nodded grimly. She had then bravely smiled and bid him farewell.

From the Goa airport, Ravi Sunderrajan went straight to the hotel to change. By 7 p.m., he was at the floating casino.

He had very little money, and his eyes were desperately looking for Valentina so that he could ask for his remaining ten lakhs.

But there was no sign of Valentina. Another hostess served him whisky, and he looked around at the faces of the people at the gambling tables, wondering if he would get a chance to play this time.

After half an hour, a man he had never seen before walked in and sat on the barstool next to him. The stranger smiled at him. Ravi looked away.

That's when he heard the man clear his throat to get Ravi's attention.

As Ravi turned to look at him, he said, 'Mr Ravi, Daku and Kallu have sent their regards.'

Ravi jumped up from the barstool, and some of the whisky from the glass he was holding spilled on his clothes.

The man said, 'Relax, keep your excitement in check.'

'Where is my money?'

'It's in the room, all ten lakhs.' The man took out a key from his pocket and gave it to him, adding, 'Cabin 207, deck 2.'

Ravi took the key and walked towards the lift. Within minutes, he was standing in front of cabin 207. He used the key and walked in. There was a black bag on the bed. He unzipped it. It had the money. He locked the room from the inside and started to count. It was ten lakhs.

Ravi then picked up the bag and left the cabin. A minute later, he was back at the gambling deck. His eyes flew to the corner where he had met the man. There was no sign of him.

Ravi relaxed. There was, after all, honour among thieves. His eyes sparkling with excitement, he exchanged five lakhs for playing chips right away.

Over the next three days, Ravi played hard but kept losing his money like always. Finally, at midnight on the third night, desperate and angry, he placed a bet for the last two lakhs in one go. Once again, he lost the money.

Depressed and lonely, he sat down in a corner, nursing his final drink of the night. As he finished his drink and placed the glass down, a familiar voice reached his ears. He turned and found Valentina standing there with a refill.

'Mr Ravi, good evening. I hope you're having a good time.'

Ravi smiled and said, 'You know everything, don't you? How are you, Valentina?'

'I'm good. Would you like to play more?'

He got up and started to walk. 'Where are Daku and Kallu? In the same meeting room?'

She placed a hand on his shoulder and stopped him. 'No, there is someone else. He wants a loan of five crores from your bank. Can you help him?'

Ravi smiled. 'Of course, and now I'm supposed to ask what's in it for you, right?'

'It's twenty thousand now.'

'I thought you would say ten thousand, like the last time.'

'That was two years ago, Ravi. You have become bigger now.'

He laughed. 'Yes, and I have never been caught.'

He followed her swinging hips to the lift.

As soon as the lift doors closed, the newsreader on the TV started to announce the arrest of Daku Singh, Kallu Singh and their three accomplices in Madhya Pradesh. But the TV was on mute.

CASE #2

WHEN THE RUBBER MEETS THE ROAD

Case overview and tools of investigation: The use of DNA profiling and 'gait analysis' from CCTV footage results in the arrest of a paedophile and murderer in Mumbai.

Location: Mumbai

Twenty-six-year-old Abdul Siddique was talking on his mobile phone as he stepped into the Nehru Nagar locality of Kurla (East) in Mumbai. The time was 9 p.m., and there were a lot of people on the road returning from work. This was a lower-middle-class neighbourhood, and the residents mostly belonged to the working class.

Abdul's eyes were wide in anticipation of what lay ahead, and a gentle smile played on his lips. A passerby would think that the reason for Abdul's smile was the conversation he was having on the phone. But the fact was Abdul's phone was off and he was merely pretending to be on a call, smiling and nodding his head from time to time.

As he walked, his eyes scanned the surroundings carefully. Five feet seven inches tall, with a wheatish complexion and a slight build, Abdul had a forgettable face.

Ten minutes later, he sighted his target. It was a five-year-old girl who was sitting under a lamppost and playing with stones. His smile widening, he approached her.

Moving the phone a few inches away from his head, he whispered to the girl, 'Hey, come on, your papa is calling you.'

The girl looked up and smiled after a moment's hesitation.

Abdul continued, 'Come fast. Papa is waiting for you with a chocolate.'

'Chocolate?' The girl threw the stones, got up and held Abdul's extended finger. He began to walk away from the spot, the phone once again against his ear.

Five minutes later, they reached an under-construction building. The girl looked up at him and asked, 'Papa? Chocolate?'

Abdul nodded towards the top of the building while pretending to be listening on the phone.

He tugged her hand forward, and the girl walked with him into the building. They climbed to the terrace of the five-floor building. Then, as they stopped, he said, '*Arre, tere kapde pe to keeda baitha hai.*' (Hey, there is an insect on your clothes.)

The girl brushed off her clothes.

Abdul said, '*Kapde ke andar chala gaya hai. Chalo, kapde nikalo jaldi se.*' (It has gone inside your clothes. Come on, take off your clothes quickly.)

The girl obeyed and was naked in a minute.

CASE #2 : WHEN THE RUBBER MEETS THE ROAD

For the next half-hour, Abdul raped the girl. After he was done, he got up and looked around. No one had heard the girl's cries—but what if someone had? What if this girl identified him later? What if the police caught him and sent him to jail? What if …?

Meanwhile, the girl regained consciousness and started to scream again. A pool of blood had formed under her, and Abdul panicked. He placed his hand over her nose and mouth. The girl was weak, but her body struggled for the next couple of minutes before falling silent.

Abdul removed his hand. It was all quiet now. He put on his trousers and looked around, his eyes wide with fear and his face shining in the dim light due to the sweat.

After a few minutes of searching, he found an empty gunny bag. He stuffed the girl's body into the bag and dragged her to the staircase area. Then he pushed the gunny bag under the staircase and covered it with bricks, stones, sandbags and other construction rubble lying in the vicinity. Satisfied, he climbed the five floors down and walked out of the building, the phone once again against his ear as if he were still having a conversation.

Vijay Kamble, DCP of Zone 6 of Mumbai police, was at his desk when the phone rang. He closed the file he was reading and picked up the phone. 'Kamble!'

The voice on the other side was edgy. 'Sir, Inspector Gawde from Nehru Nagar police station speaking.'

'Yes, Gawde?'

'Sir, a five-year-old girl's body has been found this morning at a construction site. Raped and murdered.'

Vijay took a deep breath and said, 'What's happening, Gawde? This is the third such case in, what, four months in your area?'

'Sir—'

'I don't want to hear anything. Start asking around, check CCTV footage, get the autopsy and collect the DNA. DO IT NOW!' He shouted the final three words.

'Yes, sir.'

DCP Vijay Kamble disconnected the phone and looked at the picture of his wife and six-year-old daughter that was kept on the table. He stared at the picture for a few minutes, his eyes glassy.

He knew what would happen next. Therefore, a few minutes later, he called Inspector Gawde again. 'Gawde, I want a two-hourly report.'

'Sir, two-hourly? What could I have every two hours to give you?'

'You better have something, Gawde. This was someone's daughter. Three such daughters have been raped and murdered and what are we doing? Just sitting around, waiting for the next rape and murder! I want a two-hourly report, okay?'

'Yes, sir.'

He disconnected the phone and switched on the news. Just as expected, the media was there in full force, crawling all over the under-construction building, creating all kinds of stories, making the job of the police more difficult.

CASE #2 : WHEN THE RUBBER MEETS THE ROAD

By the time he was done with his lunch, there was the phone call he knew would come. It was the DGP. The boss had chosen to bypass the hierarchy.

Without responding to DCP Kamble's greeting, the DGP started to speak. 'I got a call from the home minister just now, Kamble. *This* bastard needs to be caught before he commits another murder.'

'Yes, sir.'

'What's your plan?'

'Sir, we are combing the Nehru Nagar area, asking anyone who could have seen this animal and going through the CCTV footage too. The body has been sent for autopsy, and we will pick up the DNA samples of the criminal. There was a medical examiner at the crime scene this morning, and he has spotted semen and hair belonging to the killer. But …'

'But what?'

'I wish we could compare the DNA with the people of the area, particularly those who have a criminal record.'

'So do that. What's the problem?'

'The problem is the cost, sir. Each DNA test costs Rs 5,000.'

'You go ahead, Kamble. I will get you the financial approval. Just ask the laboratory in Santa Cruz to start their process. We *have* to catch this bastard before he strikes again.'

'Yes, sir.'

'And …' The DGP paused for a few seconds, as if making up his mind about whether he should continue or not, but then he did, his voice lowered. 'The last body was found on the terrace of the police quarters, wasn't it? Are you sure no one from our force is involved? What about the family members of the police staff from your thana?'

'Sir, we investigated that angle. I don't think anyone from our police force or their family members are involved.'

'I don't agree with you here, Kamble. I want you to check the DNA of our guys too. Clear?'

Before DCP Kamble could respond, the phone was disconnected.

Inspector Gawde had sent his entire team to the crime scene. Now, as he got up to his feet to leave the police station to monitor the progress, he heard a vehicle screech to a halt.

He stepped out and saw DCP Vijay Kamble's vehicle. He paced towards it. 'Good evening, sir.'

'Where are you going, Gawde?'

'To the crime scene, sir.'

'Come with me.'

'Yes, sir.'

Both sat in the DCP's vehicle and departed for the crime scene. During the short drive, Gawde filled the DCP in on the details of the case. He had been calling the DCP every two hours as directed too.

'So how soon can we begin the DNA comparisons?'

'Sir, there are seven lakh people in Kurla, out of which two lakh are under my police station's jurisdiction. Even with the financial sanction, since we can't compare everyone's DNA, I suggest we start with the history-sheeters first.'

CASE #2 : WHEN THE RUBBER MEETS THE ROAD

'Hmm ... but what if this is the first crime of this sadist?'

'Sir, if this is his first crime, he wouldn't be more than twenty-three or twenty-four years old, and we would have caught him by now. This guy is older and smarter, I think.'

'You have a point. So what's your plan?'

'Sir, besides history-sheeters, I also want to check younger people who are either jobless or appear suspicious. My boys will patrol the area and look for such people.'

They reached the under-construction site and stopped. Within seconds, the vehicle was surrounded by the waiting journalists.

The DCP whispered his frustration: 'This circus is the worst.'

'Sir, just give me a couple of minutes. My SI will chase them away.'

They sat inside, looking at the journalists shouting questions, ignoring them. Within a minute, the area around the vehicle was cordoned off by the SI of Nehru Nagar police station and four constables.

DCP Kamble and Inspector Gawde finally got out and took the stairs to the top floor. The crime had been committed the previous night, and everything in the vicinity must have been the same as it was now. The DCP walked to the edge of the terrace and looked down. Vehicles and pedestrians moved on the crowded road five floors below. He heard incessant honking. There was no way the screams of a five-year-old girl would have travelled that far. The adjacent buildings were far too.

After a few minutes, the DCP left for home. On his way, he called the DGP. 'Sir, I'm returning from the crime scene—'

'And? Leads?'

'As of now, we have nothing, sir.'

'When are we starting with the DNA comparisons, Kamble? I faxed a sanction for Rs 40 lakh this afternoon.'

'Sir, the samples have been collected and sent to the lab. It's our top priority.'

The DGP disconnected the phone. By now, DCP Vijay Kamble had reached the door of his flat. He pressed the bell, mumbling to himself, 'Come on, come on. I need to look happy.'

The door was opened by his six-year-old daughter. She smiled and hugged him. 'Dad, I love you.'

He hugged her back and picked her up in his arms. Then, sniffing her hair and kissing her cheek, he walked inside the house and whispered, 'I love you too, beta.'

By the time he placed his daughter down next to the dining table in the living room, his eyes had become glassy. His wife was seated on a chair. She got to her feet and came close. 'Is everything okay?'

DCP Kamble looked at her and smiled, as a teardrop rolled down his cheek. 'Yes, everything is fine.'

The result of the lab report was something the police had not expected. The finding sent them into a tizzy. Because according to the DNA analysis of the evidence found at the site of the crimes, the three rapes and murders had been carried out by two different people. While one criminal had committed the rape and murder of two girls, the other had raped and killed one girl.

CASE #2 : WHEN THE RUBBER MEETS THE ROAD

With this discovery, the questions for the police multiplied. Who were these men? Were they working together? It was highly unlikely because serial killers almost never work as a team. Were they hiding in the same area or had they escaped to other parts of Mumbai or beyond?

Over the next few weeks, Gawde's men rounded up many suspicious men from the Nehru Nagar area, including the history-sheeters, and with that the tedious and expensive process of DNA comparisons started. But over the next few months, all their efforts came to naught. The specially approved and costly police operation was turning out to be a failure.

Hiding in his house in Kurla, Abdul Siddique was a scared man. He had heard that the police were collecting DNA samples of random people. He had, therefore, stopped going out. What if the police confronted him and asked for his sample? The thought made him shiver with fear.

Abdul lived in a two-room house with his mother and three brothers, one elder to him and two younger. Another elder brother lived in Dubai.

Abdul worked for a company that made building construction material. He had studied in a convent school in Mumbai till the tenth grade and had even completed a diploma in engineering. He could, therefore, speak good English and was always turned out in neat shirts and ironed trousers.

Over the last few days, worried due to the police crackdown, a plan was beginning to form in Abdul's mind.

One day, he called up his elder brother in Dubai. 'Brother, I'm tired of working for a meagre salary in India. It's such a disgusting country.'

His brother asked, 'What do you want to do then?'

'I want to work in Dubai.'

'You have good qualifications, Abdul. But here you will have to work very hard. The employers are tough taskmasters—it's not like India.'

'I can work hard, trust me.'

'Can you do twelve-hour daily shifts?'

'Yes.'

'Okay, email me your degrees and let me see what I can do.'

Meanwhile, one day, Gawde called DCP Kamble. 'Sir, we have a situation here.'

'What is it, Gawde?'

'Sir, you remember one of the victims' bodies was found on the terrace of the police quarters?'

'Yes, so?'

'You had asked me to test the DNA samples of the policemen I suspect and their family members, sir.'

'Right.'

'Sir, I suspect my Sub-Inspector's son. He's a drug addict, and there are very good chances that he did it. Therefore, I want his DNA to be tested, but the SI is not cooperating.'

'Why? What's his problem?'

'He is insisting that his son gave up doing drugs a few months ago. He's fragile and the testing will psychologically affect him.'

'That's bullshit. Don't pay any attention to that, Gawde. I will bell the cat. Tell him I want the DNA of his son tested, and if required, we will test the DNA of all the residents of the police quarters. We can't take any chances.'

'But, sir ...'

'Either he gives his son's sample or faces suspension. Tell him this is from the DGP himself.'

'Yes, sir.'

By January 2011, within four months of the crime, more than five hundred DNA tests had been completed, but there was no breakthrough. The police had no leads and their information networks had failed. Based on people's statements, the sketches the police had prepared and widely circulated had failed to yield results too.

However, there was some solace. Owing to the increased surveillance and sustained patrolling, the serial killers had kept away, and the area seemed safe for the time being.

Then one July day in 2011, while it was raining heavily in Mumbai, Inspector Gawde received a call from the laboratory.

'Gawde speaking.'

'Sir, there is a match.'

Gawde jumped to his feet. 'Match? Who? Who is it?'

'The name is Irfan Suleman, sir. Note down the address.'

Gawde sat down and wrote the address in his diary. By the time he had placed the phone down, he was smiling.

Minutes later, Gawde sent his best team to the address and Irfan was arrested. He was nineteen years old and he confessed to the crime within minutes of interrogation.

With one rapist-killer down, DCP Kamble's nerves eased a little, and the news calmed tempers elsewhere too. The police were doing their job, the home minister made a statement and public faith was restored to some extent. The media too, for a change, praised the use of technology by the police to nab the criminal.

But one of the killers was still out there, hiding, watching and perhaps preparing to strike again. DCP Kamble, therefore, knew that they would have to keep burning the midnight oil. The DNA comparisons continued, but after a few more months, as the financial sanction ran out, the unsolved rape and murder of the remaining two minor girls turned into a cold case, and more pressing new investigations drew the police's attention. Months passed without any more leads.

Finally, in 2012, refusing to let go of the cases, DCP Kamble recommended that the cases be transferred to the CID branch of the Mumbai police, and it was approved by the DGP.

But here too, despite more tests, there was no breakthrough over the next year, and the trail turned cold. There were no further crimes using a similar modus operandi.

Meanwhile, with his brother's help, Abdul had succeeded in getting a job in Abu Dhabi. But he didn't like the long working hours, just as his brother had predicted. Also, the police were very nosy, and the punishment for any crime, however small, was too scary for him. He worked for one year, keeping his head low, biding his time, his mind all the time in Mumbai.

By 2013, when Abdul returned to Mumbai, his family had shifted from Kurla, and in the new area, the police were not asking for DNA samples. This discovery relaxed him a bit, and he started to fantasize about committing the crimes again. But going forward, he decided not to kill his victims. Killing generated too much heat.

In 2015, on a day off from his job Abdul boarded a morning train to take him outside the limits of Mumbai. One and a half hours later, he got down at Panvel. It was afternoon, and as he looked around the sleepy town, he realized he had reached a perfect hunting ground.

Holding his phone to his ear, he walked for a couple of kilometres, until he found a girl playing under a tree. She was around eight. He walked past her and checked both sides of the road to see if there was anyone watching. There was no one.

Satisfied, he approached the girl. Then, stopping a few feet from her, the phone a few inches from his ear, he whispered, 'Hey, Papa is calling you. Come.'

The girl looked at him uncertainly.

He took a step closer. 'Beta, Papa has chocolate. Come.'

She got up and walked closer to him, blinking.

'Come.' He extended his finger.

She took it and he began to take her away, his heart beating wildly. Nervousness melted away and excitement took over.

He stopped near an under-construction house. It was only two floors, but it appeared to be deserted, as if the construction had been halted a few years ago.

He smiled and said, 'Chocolate. Papa.'

The girl held back. He pulled her towards the building, but she didn't budge and just stared at him.

Abdul smiled as best as he could and whispered, 'Mumma. Chocolate.'

The girl smiled feebly and repeated, 'Mumma?'

With that, she walked into the building with him.

He took her to the first floor. It was perfect. He suddenly jumped away from her. '*Arre, kapde pe keeda hai. Kapde nikalo.*' (Hey, there's an insect on your clothes. Remove your clothes.)

The girl didn't move. Unable to bear it any longer, Abdul pulled her close and started to forcibly remove her clothes. Within seconds, she started to scream.

Before Abdul could properly undress her or himself, he heard a voice from behind him. '*Abe, yeh kya kar raha hai tu?*' (Hey, what are you doing?)

Abdul stopped and turned. All he saw was a closed fist that hit him on the nose. He fell on his back. Three young men looked down at him. While two of them began thrashing Abdul, the third helped the girl put her clothes back on.

Abdul didn't attack them back. He just lay there in the foetal position, trying to protect himself. Ten minutes later, when the men were tired, one of them called the police. By now, Abdul was bleeding from his nose and mouth. His shirt and trousers were torn and there were bruises all over his body.

The police arrested him, and he was remanded to custody.

To the investigating police officer, Abdul pleaded, 'Sahib, I was only trying to help the girl as she said she was lost.'

The officer glared at him. 'Tell me the truth, you scumbag.'

'I swear, sir. I'm innocent. I have never done anything like what you people are thinking. Check the police records. I'm a convent-educated person, sir. I'm not a criminal.'

The girl abducted by Abdul was unable to clearly state the facts to the police. Over the next two months, the police tried to convince the judge of his wrongdoing, but Abdul was allowed to walk free as there was indeed no prior criminal record against him. He also spoke to the judge in English and informed everyone that he had even travelled abroad for work. His story was that he was visiting Panvel as he wanted to explore the possibility of opening a hardware store in the city.

After Abdul was back in Mumbai, he breathed easy, but the regular beatings in the police lockup had rattled him. He knew that he was saved by the skin of his teeth and, therefore, he decided to stay away from such temptations. For the next two years, he focused only on his job and hardly interacted with his mother and brothers who stayed with him.

As he was sloppy at work, Abdul's bosses frequently fired him, and he had to shift workplaces often. To adjust, his family had to shift their house from one locality in Mumbai to the other, adjusting to the ebb and flow of the combined earnings of the brothers. Finally, by 2017, the family had settled in Bhayandar, at the northern end of Mumbai.

Then one day, in the same year, Abdul read about the conviction of Irfan Suleman, the nineteen-year-old man who was arrested six years ago for the rape and murder in Nehru Nagar based on DNA matching. Irfan was sentenced to life, and the news sent a chill down Abdul's spine. With this, he found another reason to throttle the beast within him and promised once more to himself that he would stay focused on his job. But he had no idea that within a few months, the animal within him would take over his mind.

In 2017, when a very competent IPS officer by the name of Vishal Kumar took over the CID office, the rapes of minors started again. Cases were being reported every week, but there were no murders, only molestations. And this time, the victims were older girls, in the age group of ten to thirteen. Since the crimes were being committed all over the city, panic spread fast.

As the cases kept mounting, so did the efforts of the CID. The victims were questioned at length by sensitive female police officers. The people present in the vicinity of the crime, who might have seen the criminal, were questioned by the police too. Slowly, a picture began to emerge and a few facts stood out. One, the perpetrator was always on phone; two, he was seen wearing spotless, full-sleeved shirts and trousers; and three, he was pleasant in his mannerisms and seemed educated because he spoke good English.

These findings, however, were not enough to catch the criminal. The CID needed more. Vishal and his team then turned to CCTV. Hours and hours of CCTV footage were scrutinized from the vicinity of the crimes, but the videos were of poor quality. Meanwhile, the molestations continued. There were no murders, though, as the victims were let off after the crime.

One afternoon, a team member called up Vishal Kumar. 'Sir, I think we have found our target.'

The image was emailed to him moments later, and Vishal Kumar took a printout and pinned it on the board in his office. It was a hazy image of a man in a full-sleeved shirt and creased trousers talking on a phone.

He called back. 'How are you sure it is him?'

'Sir, at almost all the locations, the CCTV shows this man near the crime scene. It has to be him. The peculiar thing is that he is always on the phone.'

'Who is he talking to? Check the call logs for these locations.'

'Sir, we have already done that. It appears that he is not talking on the phone. He's only pretending to be talking on the phone.'

Vishal Kumar reclined in his high-back leather chair and spoke his mind after a few moments. 'Oh, so talking on the phone is his *getaway*. No one pays attention to people who are on the phone. Smart!'

'Yes, sir.'

'Do we know the local train he takes?'

'Always towards Virar, sir.'

'Looking for him on that route would be like looking for a needle in a haystack. But we've got to start somewhere. Make six teams and go with this image to ask people if they have seen him.'

Two weeks later, a man in Mira Road, a locality near Bhayandar, recognized the CID's suspect. Minutes later, they were knocking on the door of Abdul's house.

Abdul's mother opened the door. She frowned at the plainclothed CID investigators and demanded, 'What do you want?'

They showed her the printout and said, 'We want to talk to Abdul Siddique.'

She stood there for a few moments, uncertain, until Abdul walked to the door, asking, 'Who is it, Mother?'

The CID inspectors recognized him instantly. 'You are under arrest for rape and murder, Abdul.'

Abdul just stood there, staring at the men who were holding his picture in their hands. He was handcuffed and taken away as his mother screamed in the background, 'This is a mistake, sahib! My Abdul is innocent.'

During the initial questioning in the lockup, Abdul remained passive and said over and over again, 'Sir, I don't know anything about these crimes. I'm just a salesman who travels a lot.'

When the police were unable to crack him, Vishal asked his team to bring him to his room at the CID headquarters. Meanwhile, Vishal had spent hours studying the CCTV clippings of Abdul walking near the scenes of the crimes. He, therefore, had a plan.

After Abdul was brought to Vishal Kumar's office, Vishal got down to business straightaway.

'What were you doing near the locations where these minor girls were molested?'

'Sir, I don't know anything about the molestations. I'm a salesman and I have to travel a lot for work.' Abdul was surprisingly calm.

'Okay, I want you to get up and walk up to that wall.' He pointed to the opposite end of the room.

Abdul hesitated, but he got up and walked towards the wall.

'Now turn around and look at me.'

He obeyed.

'Start walking towards me now.'

Abdul walked with a slight limp, his left arm hardly moving from his side.

Vishal Kumar had all he needed. 'Okay, you can go now.'

Abdul looked uncertain. He was taken away.

Vishal Kumar then called the team leader of his investigating team and said, 'Send his DNA sample and ask the lab guys to compare it with the Nehru Nagar samples from 2010.'

'Yes, sir.'

A day later, the laboratory had a perfect match. The CID finally had their man. The DNA nailed him as the one responsible for the two murders, and the gait analysis (the study of how someone walks) and his presence near the locations of the molestations as captured by CCTVs connected him to these crimes. With that, the state had an impregnable case. In all, fifteen molestations were proved besides the two murders, and Abdul was sent to prison.

It was during the search of Abdul's house in Bhayandar that the newspaper clippings of Irfan's arrest and conviction were discovered. Abdul had been following the case closely. The police also found the documents from his arrest and subsequent release from the Panvel case.

Abdul was smart. He was calm, calculated and knew how to stay under the police's radar. But finally, the police beat him by using technology and working overtime. The fact that the laboratory had preserved the 2010 DNA samples till 2017, despite a massive workload, once again proved why the Mumbai police is considered a top-class professional organization.

CASE #3

BACK AGAINST THE WALL

Case overview and tools of investigation: The use of sustained IMEI tracking and DNA matching by forensic experts of the Kerala police led to the successful capture and conviction of a migrant labourer responsible for the rape and murder of a law student.

Location: Kerala, Assam and Tamil Nadu

Jamaluddin Islam stopped on the pebbled dirt track. It was 5 p.m., and he was barely a hundred feet away from his destination. Although he was drunk, Jamaluddin knew he had to be careful. He looked to his left and right, checking for any passersby. There was no one in sight.

Jamaluddin was five feet and seven inches tall, dark-complexioned and skinny. A migrant labourer from Assam who had made Kerala his home for almost a decade, he could speak Malayalam fluently.

As he started walking, excited at the prospect of what lay ahead, he began to hum a song.

He was wearing a yellow shirt, loose trousers and rubber slippers. His well-oiled hair was disheveled, and a mixture of dirt and sweat had made patterns on his face. He was carrying a half-finished bottle of cheap whisky in his left hand, and he had hidden a 20-inch knife in the hip pocket of his trousers, covered by the loose shirt.

A few minutes later, he could see the entrance of his target's one-room house. A smile spread across his face as he murmured, 'I will make you mine today, Jaya … mine forever.'

Before moving towards the door, he looked around one final time. The other houses were scattered fifty to a hundred feet from one another. This was an area where poor people lived, and he knew it was early for them to return to their homes. There was no one around.

The year was 2017, and it was March, the hottest month in Kerala. Wiping the sweat from his forehead using the sleeve of his shirt, Jamaluddin started to move again. When he reached the door, he paused briefly, wondering if he should knock. On second thought, he placed his ear against the wooden door and frowned in concentration. There was no sound. He knew Jaya was alone in the house.

Slowly, he pushed the door. It was open, and it swung inwards. He stepped inside.

'Who is it?' He heard Jaya's voice.

Jamaluddin's eyes scanned the room and adjusted to the dim light within just a second. Jaya was sitting on a stool in one corner, an empty steel plate kept by her side on the floor. It looked like she had just finished eating.

'Sweetheart, it's your lover,' he whispered.

Jaya jumped to her feet. She knew this man. He had stopped her many times on her way home from college, but she had never spoken to him. He used to whistle, pass lewd comments and scare her into giving up, threatening to kill her if she didn't. But Jaya was not scared of people like Jamaluddin. Even at this moment, she was certain he could do nothing.

Jaya took a step towards him and said, 'If you don't want me to scream, leave right now.'

Jamaluddin laughed. 'I have come here to fuck you, my queen. Why don't you just lie down and lift your legs.'

Jaya was uncertain what to do next. The man in front of her was drunk—she could see a bottle of whisky in his hand. *I should just overpower him and throw him out of the house before calling the police*, she thought.

Twenty-nine-year-old Jaya had always been a quiet but courageous girl. She was studying law in a college nearby, and her plan was to start practising as a lawyer as soon as she got her degree. That was the only way she could earn enough to construct a decent house for her family and protect them from the unruly people of the village. Her younger sister, Reva, was not interested in studying further and, therefore, Jaya's next step after the house was ready was to marry her off in grand style. She also wanted to stop her mother, Bhagyashri, from doing the menial daily-wage jobs that she had been doing all her life. The family had strained relations with Ramu, Jaya and Reva's father, who stayed all by himself in a house around a kilometre away.

Jamaluddin unscrewed the cap of the whisky bottle. Then, as his eyes locked with Jaya's, he brought the bottle close to his mouth and took a few sips.

'This is my final warning,' declared Jaya, her voice a bit uncertain now. The way he was looking at her was beginning to scare her.

Jaya looked around, wondering if there was something with which she could defend herself. There was nothing. The man who was about to attack her was standing between her and the door. Escape was not possible, unless she brought the man down. Since he was swaying due to drunkenness, Jaya thought she could fight him off.

Jamaluddin took a few more sips. Then he kept the bottle on the floor and started to take off his shirt. After he had thrown his shirt to one side, he started to take off his trousers.

'Stop. I want you to leave right now.' Jaya was surprised at how she sounded.

Jamaluddin laughed again.

Something fell to the floor with a clank as he took off his trousers. Jamaluddin stopped laughing and bent down to pick up the knife.

Jaya opened her mouth to scream, but Jamaluddin leapt on her in an instant, plunging the knife into her torso in one swift motion. Jaya fell backwards, the blade of the knife embedded in her body as Jamaluddin fell on top of her.

Jaya was in a state of shock due to the excruciating pain. Reflexively, she struggled to throw her attacker off her. After a few moments of struggle, as Jamaluddin tried to remove her clothes, she succeeded in wriggling away from under him.

CASE #3 : BACK AGAINST THE WALL

Looking down at the blood that was oozing from under her shoulder blade, she pressed it with both her hands.

Before she could decide what to do next, Jamaluddin jumped and sat on top of her. Then, as she crossed her hands to protect her face, he drove the knife into her neck. She fought back, her occasional punches hitting her attacker feebly. By now, her survival instinct had taken over and she was shaking her body with all her might; her hands and legs were hitting anything they could.

But Jamaluddin didn't stop attacking her. He continued slicing and puncturing her until Jaya had reached a vegetative state. She was not dead, but she could no longer move or fight back.

Jamaluddin took off her clothes now, and when she was fully naked, he raped her. When he was done, he heard a whisper.

'Water. Water, please …' Jaya was mumbling.

Jamaluddin laughed. 'I don't have water, only whisky.'

With that, he poured whisky into her partially open mouth, and as she choked due to the liquid, he laughed hysterically.

But the madman was not done yet. Even though his sexual appetite was sated the animal in him wasn't. He picked up the knife and approached his victim once again.

Jaya saw him through half-open eyes, her body bleeding from so many places. That's when Jamaluddin inserted the entire knife into the victim's private parts and started to dismember her. He went on for several minutes, not bothering to check if Jaya was dead or alive.

When he was finally tired, or bored, or both, he got up and looked around the room. His clothes were lying on the floor.

He picked them up and got dressed. The effort of the violence had diluted his drunkenness, and his brain was more alert now. Jamaluddin didn't want to leave any evidence, so he picked up the knife and the bottle.

Satisfied, he opened the door and peeped out. It was 6.30 p.m. and there was no one in sight. He stepped out, shut the door behind him and rushed away from the house, careful not to take the path used by people. A few minutes later, he reached a canal, where he washed away the blood from the exposed parts of his body. He threw the empty whisky bottle and knife into the canal.

Ten minutes later, Jamaluddin was almost a kilometre from the victim's house, standing on the main road that led to Kochi. He was looking for a lift.

Jamaluddin was calm, and he was smiling. There was no nervousness, no doubt and, of course, no remorse.

He waved to a truck, and when it stopped, he said, 'Just a five-kilometre lift.'

'Get in,' the driver said.

Within minutes into the drive, Jamaluddin was cracking jokes and the driver was laughing uncontrollably.

'Stop here.'

The truck stopped, and Jamaluddin jumped out. 'Thank you.'

He waited for the truck to go out of sight before stepping onto the narrow pathway that branched off from the main road. After a five-minute walk, he reached a small cluster of huts. This was a migrant labourers' colony, with twenty-odd temporary huts and sheds packed onto a small piece of land.

The sun had set by now, but there was enough light. Hens ran around as kids chased them with sticks, women washed clothes using buckets of collected water and smoke seeped through the joints and edges of the roofs of the huts.

Jamaluddin knew what he had to do next. Although there were no witnesses and the victim was already dead, he thought it was best for him to leave the state of Kerala once and for all. With this in mind, he moved towards the hut that belonged to him.

Fifty-five-year-old Bhagyashri approached her house at half-past eight the same evening. Her younger daughter, Reva, was with her. They were returning home after toiling at a construction site for the whole day and both were hungry.

As Bhagyashri pushed the door open, all she had on her mind was the food that she knew her elder daughter, Jaya, would have prepared for her and Reva.

The door swung inwards. The room was dark, and her first thought was that Jaya had gone to sleep. Maybe she had had a tiring day at the college, Bhagyashri thought, as she reached for the light switch and flicked it on.

The room was bathed in yellow light, and there she was, right in the middle of the room, a heap of blood, flesh and torn clothes.

Bhagyashri screamed and collapsed next to her daughter. Reva screamed too. The two of them cried for fifteen minutes, their minds refusing to understand and accept what they were seeing. None of the neighbours approached their house to ask what the matter was. Perhaps the distance had been too much for the sound to carry, or perhaps they didn't want to have anything to do with the mother and the sisters.

Finally, Bhagyashri turned to Reva, her face firm, and said, 'Call the police.'

Reva nodded and dialled 100.

Circle Inspector P. David was the first to arrive at the crime scene, along with Sub-Inspector Gautham Nair and two constables, Shankar M. and Mohan Jayakumar. The time was 9 p.m.

He got out of the jeep and looked around. Some people who lived in the nearby houses had heard their vehicle screech to a halt and had stepped out to see what was happening.

David knew there would be a crowd of curious bystanders soon. This was expected and sometimes proved to be useful.

He turned towards Shankar. 'Stay here! You know what to do.'

Shankar saluted and said, 'Yes, sir.'

David turned, and the other two followed him as he walked towards the victim's house. Since the path was unlit and it was dark now, Mohan overtook David quickly and used his phone's torch to show the way.

As they approached the house, the police team could hear cries of pain and despair. The door was open, and David stepped inside. He first looked around to assess the crime scene.

The older woman turned to look at the three policemen in uniform and started to cry more bitterly. Then she tried to get up on her feet but couldn't.

David spoke in Malayalam. 'My name is Inspector David. Who called 100?'

Reva looked at him and said, 'I did.'

David asked her, 'What's your name?'

'Reva.'

'Is this your mother?'

'Yes, and her name is Bhagyashri.'

Bhagyashri, on hearing her name, started to cry loudly again.

'I'm sorry for your loss ... What's the victim's name?'

'Jaya, sir.'

'Okay, did anyone come here from the time you called the police till now?'

'No, sir.'

'Look, this is a crime scene now. I want you two to slowly move away and out of this room. The forensic team will be here soon.'

Reva nodded and helped her mother to her feet. With that, Sub-Inspector Nair and Constable Mohan cautiously approached the body. It was a gruesome sight, and instinctively, they pulled out their handkerchiefs and their hands flew to cover their noses.

As Reva and Bhagyashri reached the door, they sat down next to it.

David shook his head. 'No, no, not there. I meant out of the house. Go to the neighbour's house and wait there.'

Mother and daughter looked at one another and then Bhagyashri spoke in a low voice. 'We can't go to anyone's house. No one will take us in.'

'I'll send a constable and I assure you they will.'

'No, please. We are from the Scheduled Caste, sir. They don't treat us well. We will sit outside our house and we won't interfere with your work.'

'Okay.' With that Inspector David turned and went to his team members.

Both looked up at him as they heard him approach.

'What do we have here?' asked David.

Sub-Inspector Nair replied, 'Sir, looks like rape and murder of the kind I have not seen in my ten-year' career so far. This is the work of an animal.'

David nodded and sat on his haunches for a closer look. The three of them heard more footsteps near the door.

The forensics team had arrived.

By now, the neighbours outside had formed a circle around the house, and with each passing minute, they were edging closer to find out more details.

Constable Shankar knew he had an important job to do. Without looking curious, he started to observe the people standing there. There were around twenty now, mostly men but a few women too. He knew, over time, this number would grow. Since the light was dim and he didn't want to miss anything, Shankar got inside the jeep and turned the ignition and the headlights on.

His phone started to ring just then. It was his boss, Inspector David.

'Yes, sir?'

'Shankar, this is one of the worst rape-and-murder cases we have seen. I'm sure it is the work of someone who's either a serial killer or a lunatic. Observe the people closely. Serial killers like to watch what the police is doing.'

'Yes, sir.'

Shankar pocketed the phone, climbed out of the jeep and got back to his observation. The jeep lights had improved visibility. After a few minutes, his eyes locked with those of a middle-aged man who was wearing a lungi and a vest. For a moment, nothing happened, and then the man shifted his body weight from one foot to the other. Shankar kept his eyes on him and the man started to feel uncomfortable. He lowered his eyes and after a few seconds, when the man slowly raised them again, Shankar was still looking at him. This made him very conscious and nervous.

The man stepped back, turned and started to walk away.

'Hey!' shouted Shankar and started to walk towards him.

The man began to run when he saw the policeman following him. Shankar broke into a run as well. Within a few minutes, being much fitter, Shankar caught up with him. He pulled the man by his vest, but the tattered piece of clothing gave way, and the man fell to the ground, his lungi riding up his thigh.

'Who are you?' Shankar asked.

The man got up, adjusted his lungi and extended his hand. Shankar returned his torn vest, which was still in his hand.

The man stammered as he spoke: 'Sir, I will tell you what I saw … but … but on the condition that you will not take me to the police station.'

'Shut up and speak,' scolded Shankar.

'Sir, I saw a man running away from the hut in the evening.'

'What time and what did he look like?'

'I think around six, sir. I didn't check the exact time. He was wearing a yellow shirt and trousers.'

'What else? Did he see you?'

'No, sir, I don't think so. And he was wearing slippers.'

'Think deeply. Was he carrying something in his hand?'

'Yes, he was, but I'm not sure what it was.'

'What's your name?'

'Sir, I'm Swamy.'

'Swamy, after we round up the suspects, do you think you will be able to identify him?'

'Not sure, sir. I was very far.'

'Okay, give me your mobile number.'

After noting down Swamy's number, Shankar returned to the jeep. There were close to thirty people now. He looked at the new faces. Nothing suspicious.

Inside the house, the forensics team had photographed the crime scene in detail and collected fingerprints, hair strands and blood samples.

As Bhagyashri signed their documents, she kept saying over and over again, 'I want you to catch the bastard who did this to my child and hang him.'

The body was thereafter taken to the ambulance and driven to the medical college for an autopsy.

Shankar saw David, Nair and Mohan approach him.

David lit a cigarette and asked, 'All okay?'

Shankar replied, 'Sir, we have a witness.' He shared the information about Swamy.

After Shankar had stopped speaking, David turned towards Nair. 'Make sure our sketch artist speaks to the witness and prepares a sketch immediately. Since the poor girl is already dead, this might be our only straw of hope.'

By then, it was eleven at night, but before leaving, David wanted more information. He asked his team members to ask around while he sat in the jeep and smoked, his eyes glassy. After his team got busy and a few minutes had elapsed, he called the Superintendent under whom his circle functioned. It was time to update the boss.

'Good evening, sir.'

'Good evening, David. What have you got?'

'Sir, a rape and murder. Work of a madman, maybe a serial killer.'

'Go on.'

'We have a witness, but he says he saw the killer only from a distance. The woman was brutally murdered with at least two dozen knife wounds that I could count and her intestines pulled out. We will get more information in a few hours, after the autopsy is done.'

The SP replied, 'Okay. Do you think this is the work of one of the migrant labourers?'

'Difficult to say at the moment, sir, but it could be.'

'That's my worry, David. The locals are anyway against the migrants. I just hope we don't have an ugly backlash.'

'Yes, sir.'

'Be careful about what you say and stay away from the media. If anyone calls, ask them to speak to my public relation officer. We will release information carefully.'

'Yes, sir.'

After the forensic team took away Jaya's body, Bhagyashri and Reva went inside the house. Both of them sat quietly side by side.

At midnight, Reva's phone rang. She picked it up and said, 'Hello?'

'Hello, what happened to Jaya? I called her number and a policeman picked up the phone. He won't tell me anything. Where is she? I hope she's alright.'

Reva started to cry into the phone.

The caller continued, 'Wait, why are you crying? I'm her friend calling from Kochi. My name is Shanti. You are Reva, aren't you? Why don't you say something? Jaya gave me your number a while ago … Hello?'

'Our Jaya is gone … She's dead.'

'Dead? How? No … This is not possible.'

'Jaya was raped and killed by a monster,' Reva shouted and broke down completely, her phone slipping out of her hand.

Two medical students, under the supervision of a surgeon, carried out the autopsy. Jaya had a total of thirty stab wounds on her body. Part of her intestines were outside her body, and there was a lot of bleeding from her private parts. There was some residue of recently eaten rice and dal in her stomach, and there was some whisky in her throat, mouth and trachea. She had lost her life due to heavy bleeding caused by the knife cuts.

The surgeon knew they had to work fast and collect the samples for further examination because the family members would start demanding the body soon. After their preliminary investigation was over, the team collected saliva, blood samples, hair and scalp samples, nail clippings and a vaginal swab and secured the body in a body bag. To conclude the autopsy, more tests would be carried out with the help of these samples in the days to come.

In the hostel of the law college where Jaya studied, Shanti had informed their common friends and they had gathered in Shanti's room. It was 1 a.m. by now, and there were nine of them, including Shanti.

Shanti spoke first. 'Listen, the police will not do anything unless there is pressure on them.'

One of them replied, 'I agree, but what can we do?'

Everyone nodded, their faces serious.

Shanti said, 'The state elections are around the corner. We can put pressure on the government by starting a social media campaign.'

'I don't understand—how will that help? We are just students, after all,' another girl said.

'*Because* we are students, we can do a lot. We owe it to our friend Jaya.' Everyone waited as Shanti took a pause before continuing. 'Hashtag Justice for Jaya. Let's start this campaign on Twitter and Facebook right away.'

Shanti picked up her phone, opened the X and started to type: 'Jaya T, a student of govt law college, Kochi, was brutally raped & murdered today at her home when she was alone. The police have no leads. We demand #JusticeforJaya.'

She attached a picture of Jaya that she had on her phone and posted the message. Then she looked at her friends and they started sharing her post from their phones. Within minutes, the nine of them started calling their other friends, and requesting them to share it further.

An hour later, Shanti informed her friends, 'We should do this the whole night. The hashtag should turn viral and so big by morning that when the chief minister wakes up, this is the first thing he notices. Then, my friends, only then, can there be enough pressure on the police to catch the culprit.'

Everyone nodded and they got back to calling more people.

Earlier, at around 9 p.m., Jamaluddin had boarded the Trivandrum-Silchar express train from Kochi for Guwahati. He had bought a ticket for the general compartment, and after placing his suitcase that had all his belongings on an empty seat, he had moved towards the toilet. The train started to move just then, and it turned his smile wider.

Once inside the toilet, he latched the door and took out a new bottle of whisky from his pocket. After gulping a few mouthfuls, he opened his phone and removed the SIM card. The train was now zipping through the night at high speed. Jamaluddin bent down and peered into the darkness through the hole of the Indian commode. He tossed the SIM card into it, knowing it would fall among the stones between the tracks and no one would ever find the card—his only connection to Kerala.

After this, he raised the bottle to his mouth and continued to drink till the bottle was half finished. Then he returned to his seat. After dinner, as soon as someone got down from the compartment at a station, he spotted a top berth. Jamaluddin picked up his suitcase and placed it to one side; he went to sleep, a smile on his lips.

He would reach Guwahati two days later, from where he planned to take a bus for Lakhimpur, the city where his parents lived. He had enough cash with him, besides some savings in the bank, to last him for a couple of months. After that, his plan was to look for a job, but not in Kerala this time. He had the states of Tamil Nadu and Karnataka on his mind.

The efforts of Shanti and her friends paid off. By next morning, the issue had become huge. From activists and film stars to opposition parties and social media influencers, everyone was talking about #JusticeforJaya.

At eleven that morning, the CM asked his personal secretary to connect him to the Director General of Police (DGP). As soon as he came on the line, the CM said, 'Kumar, what is this #JusticeforJaya case? I want a briefing by 2 p.m. in my office along with the progress report.'

'Good morning, sir. Sure, sir. Just to brief you, I'm setting up a Special Investigative Team and will put my best team in action right away. Can I tell you briefly about the case, sir?'

The CM snapped, 'I know what has happened, Kumar. I want action. What have you done so far? You have three hours. See you in my office at 2.'

At the police headquarters, the DGP slowly placed the phone down. This was going to be a nightmare, he knew, given that the elections were just days away. But he also knew that he could trust his team.

He called his PA and asked him to connect him to the Additional Director General of Police (ADGP) who was in charge of the Kochi area.

As soon as he came on the line, the DGP said, 'Ram, for this Jaya case, I want you to immediately form an SIT that will operate under your overall supervision. Okay?'

'Yes, sir.'

'I want a minimum of forty police personnel, divided into ten teams, to look at every aspect of the case closely. And I want a report three times every day. At 9 a.m., 2 p.m. and 9 p.m.'

'Yes, sir.'

'Do you have any additional information besides the witness who gave a vague description?'

'No, sir. But we are working on it.'

'Ram, the CM has summoned me to his office at 2 p.m. It's almost noon. I want you to call me at 1.45 with the confirmation that the SIT has been formed and with the progress we have made.'

'Yes, sir.'

'And one more thing—speak to the medical college personally. I don't want them to leak any information to the press. Clear?'

'Yes, sir.'

The DGP slammed the phone down and cursed loudly. 'Who are you, Mr Yellow Shirt? Wherever you are hiding, we will catch you.'

Inspector David found his name in the just-constituted SIT. He smiled. The members of his team, who were the first responders at the crime scene with him, were also in the SIT. This was a good sign, as it meant that while they could keep working, there would be others to augment their efforts too.

Within the SIT, Inspector David's team was tasked with interrogating the people who lived in the vicinity of the victim's house. Over the next few days, therefore, David and his team questioned over one hundred people, working almost fifteen hours each day. The ADGP was personally monitoring the case, and he had been calling him several times a day. On the fifth day, David's team had their second breakthrough.

As David was asking questions to a man in his thirties, a young boy who was around fifteen came running towards them.

'Sir, sir, look here. There is blood on this.'

David was sitting in a cane chair. He shot up and turned his attention to what the boy was holding in his hand. It was a rubber slipper with brownish marks on it.

'Keep it here.' He pointed to the floor next to his feet. 'What makes you think this is blood?'

'What else could it be, sir? It looks like blood, I think. It *is* blood.' The boy was confident.

'Where did you find it?'

'A two-minute walk behind Jaya didi's house, on the way to the canal.'

'What's your name?'

'Joseph.'

'Okay, Joseph, thank you. You can go now.'

The boy was slightly surprised by his abrupt dismissal, but he slowly walked away.

David called the forensics team. 'We found a slipper from behind the house. Looks like it has blood marks on it.'

Thereafter, David returned to the police station. Then he sent Constable Mohan to the forensics lab, which was located in Kochi. An hour later, the rubber slipper had been deposited.

In his office, David leaned back in his chair and stared at the ceiling. This case was indeed nerve-wracking. One of the most surprising parts was that the attacker seemed to have no motive. The victim was poor and had no valuables. If the motive was only to have sex, why was she given such inhuman treatment? Was the criminal known to her? Was this his first crime? At the moment, he had no answers.

The DNA that was picked up from bite marks on the victim's body and from the door handle did not match with the database of criminals that the police had. This meant the criminal had committed his first crime in the state. But the manner in which it was executed did not make it look like one.

CASE #3 : BACK AGAINST THE WALL

The result of the DNA sampling from the blood on the slippers—if indeed it was blood—would take at least twenty-four hours to come. They had nothing else to do at the moment, except keep asking questions.

Sub-Inspector Nair entered his office.

'Nair, what have you got?'

'Sir, nothing.'

'Sit down.'

'Thank you, sir.'

'You interviewed the victim's father, didn't you?'

'I did, sir.'

'Do you think he could be involved in any way? Because his daughters had sided with their mother, and now we know that the mother's character is, well ... I don't know how much to believe, though.'

'I don't think the father is involved, sir. He seems to be struggling with his own health issues. About the victim's mother's character, I am also not sure how much to believe. Maybe people are targeting her because she's from a Scheduled Caste.'

'Possible. We have seen such instances in the past. But where is the killer hiding? How can he just disappear?'

David's phone started to ring.

'Yes, sir.'

He listened for a few minutes and then hung up.

'Who was it, sir?'

'The SP incharge of the cyber cell. I think we have a lead.'

'What is it, sir?'

'The cyber cell had been monitoring all the calls made or received through the tower that covered the area of the victim's house that night. It's a large area, and they had to go through thousands of calls. But one particular number that was active in the area disappeared the same night around 10 p.m. Want to know from where?'

'From where?'

'The SIM was apparently thrown from a train. Our cyber team found it on the railway tracks.'

'So do we have a name now?'

'Jamaluddin Islam.'

'That means we also have an address.'

'That's right.'

Both cops realized the sequence of events now. A person named Jamaluddin committed the crime, then went to Kochi and boarded the train. Now the question was which train? It wouldn't be hard for the cyber team to find out because they now had a geographical location and time. Using these two variables, they could easily find out which train passed that point at that time.

By now, it was one at night and David decided to call it a day. The two of them said good night to one another and left the police station.

Jamaluddin was using a new SIM at his parents' home in Lakhimpur, Assam. It had been one week since his arrival, and he was beginning to get bored. There were too many restrictions at home. He could not drink alcohol, he could not watch blue films freely and he was not allowed to hang out with his friends till late. On top of that, his parents wanted him to get married.

One day, Jamaluddin received a call from one of his friends in Tamil Nadu.

'Jamaluddin, brother, how are you?'

'I'm good, but getting bored.'

'Why don't you go back to Kerala? You like that job, don't you?'

'I don't want to go back there.'

'Why? Have they fired you?'

'No ... just like that. Can you help me get a job where you live?'

'Are you sure? I live in Kanchipuram and the salary here is much lower.'

'I have saved some money, so the salary is not a problem. Just get me a job.'

'Sure. I will call you in a day or two.'

Jamaluddin disconnected the phone. He was sitting under a tree not far from his house. As soon as he placed his phone in his pocket, he saw a police jeep stop in front of his house. This was not good. Two cops got out and knocked on the door.

His father opened the door and had a brief conversation with the policemen. After that, the policemen went and sat in the jeep to wait. Jamaluddin got up and silently began to walk away, his back towards the police jeep.

He was sweating now. After a few minutes, his phone started to ring. It was his father. He had shared the new number only with his parents and a few friends. He didn't accept the call, and instead, he opened the phone and took out the SIM card. After throwing it away, he checked how much money he had in his wallet. He had close to two thousand rupees. It was enough. He decided to buy a new SIM now and not share the number with anyone.

ADGP Ram was on a call with the SP of the cyber cell.

'What do you mean he wasn't at home?'

'Sir, that's what the Assam police has informed us. They went to his house, but he wasn't there, and now it has been more than twenty-four hours, but he has not returned home.'

'That's because the policemen must have told him.'

'Sir, he's on the run again, but we have him on our radar because we have his IMEI number now.'

'Good job. But how did you get that?'

'From his bill. So far, he's changed the SIM card three times.'

'Where is he now? Can we catch him by tomorrow? The DGP is under a lot of pressure from the CM. The elections start tomorrow, and the opposition has not spared a single opportunity to say that the criminal will not be caught till their government is in power.'

'Sir, looking at the quickly changing towers, we know that our man is travelling by train. But the problem is that by IMEI we can find the tower but not his exact location, and if we try to alert the police at the enroute railway stations, he will get a whiff and this time, who knows, he might throw his phone and we might lose the IMEI.'

'What do you suggest then?'

'Sir, let him reach his destination. Then we can start closing in.'

'Okay, I agree with you. I will inform the DGP accordingly.'

It was midnight when Jamaluddin arrived at his friend's place in Kanchipuram in Tamil Nadu. Even though he had bought a new SIM in Guwahati, he had only called one of his friends and asked him to inform his father that he was fine and they should not look for him, adding that the police wanted to wrongly implicate him in a case just because he was poor and he was a Muslim.

But Jamaluddin had resisted calling his friend in Kanchipuram during the entire train journey.

Now he stood facing a tin shed on the edge of Kanchipuram city, alcohol on his breath and a smile on his face. His friend was fast asleep. He knocked again and swore at him loudly.

His friend finally opened the door. He was surprised, but a moment later, he laughed and ushered him inside.

'What took you so long to open, brother?' Jamaluddin asked as he sat down on the floor.

There was no furniture, just a mattress against one of the walls and a single-burner gas stove on the opposite side.

'What do you expect me to do at midnight? I was sleeping.'

'I was thinking you were fucking a young girl.'

'Who would come here, brother?'

Jamaluddin took out the bottle from his pocket and extended it towards him. 'Here, take a few sips.'

The man shook his head. 'This is haram. In fact, as a Muslim, even you should not drink.'

'Okay, okay, keep your advice to yourself.'

The man, who had been standing, sat down on his mattress. Then he said, 'I was trying to call you yesterday, but it said the number is not valid.'

'That's because I've changed my number.'

'Changed your number? This is the third time ... Why are you changing your number? What about the remaining talk-time balance? Give me those SIMs; at least I can make some free calls.' The man smiled.

'I don't have those SIMs. Don't ask so many questions; just tell me if you got me a job or not.'

The man smiled. 'Of course. That was why I was calling you.'

Jamaluddin inhaled deeply and said, 'That's good.'

'Let's sleep now, I have to go early tomorrow.'

'You sleep, brother. I was sleeping in the bloody train for the last two days. I will just sit here.'

'Okay.'

After the man fell asleep, Jamaluddin looked at his face carefully and wondered if his friend would rat him out. But his friend had no idea what Jamaluddin had done. He tried to convince himself that he was safe in this new town and he would start a new job the next day. Moreover, his SIM was new, and even his parents didn't know the number. As long as he kept a low profile and focused on his job, he knew he would be safe.

David received a call the next morning when he was briefing his team. It was from the medical college.

'Sir, is it Inspector David?'

'Yes.'

'We have completed the DNA test on the blood marks on the rubber slipper.'

'And?'

'It matches the DNA from the bite marks on the victim's body and the blood marks on the door handle.'

'So it's the same person.'

'Yes, sir.'

'Thank you.'

David looked at his team and shared what he had just learnt.

David turned to Nair and asked, 'Did you check with the cyber team where that monster is now?'

'Yes, sir. He's now in Kanchipuram.'

'Good—we need to go and get the bastard here.'

'Right, sir. But we only know the tower's location, not the criminal's location.'

It was 10 a.m. and the counting of votes had started. The early trends showed that the ruling party was doing poorly. A change in political party in the state meant transfers for the top policemen. But this was expected, and they knew they had no control over it.

Three days later, David learnt that the ADGP incharge of the case had been changed. A woman took over the reins from him, and everyone knew that the orders had come directly from the new CM's office.

The new ADGP committed more police officers to the case, and the SIT swelled from 40 to 100. Also, at every level, the pressure was being felt to act faster. By now, most of the case had been solved. They knew the name of the criminal, and they also knew where he was hiding. The evidence was clear. If the man was arrested, his DNA would be matched against the available pieces of evidence, and once that was done, the police would have a watertight case. The new ADGP and the new government had literary nothing to do except reap the rewards.

Two days later, by the time David and his team left for Kanchipuram, the Tamil Nadu police had already been informed and had assured their full cooperation.

As they were travelling, another development was taking place in Kanchipuram. Jamaluddin's friend had begun to doubt his friend. On top of that, Jamaluddin was drinking every day and making fun of his friend's austere lifestyle.

One day, therefore, Jamaluddin's friend took an hour off from work and went to a police station. There, he told the inspector that he suspected that his friend had committed a crime either in Kerala or in Assam. The inspector asked him the suspect's name and if he had a picture. He had clicked a picture of a sleeping Jamaluddin, and he shared it with the inspector. Then, after leaving his mobile number with the inspector, he went back to work. By doing this, he felt guilt-free. If Jamaluddin had indeed done something wrong, the police would know where to look, and if he hadn't, there was nothing to worry about.

CASE #3 : BACK AGAINST THE WALL

The evening of the day Jamaluddin's friend informed the police inspector, David and his team reached the police commissioner's office in Kanchipuram. Before leaving, David had emailed the suspect's picture to the Tamil Nadu DGP in Chennai. He was confident that the picture must have been emailed to all the police stations in Kanchipuram city.

The police commissioner met the Kerala officers in the conference room. There was an SP with him and a couple of ACPs.

The police commissioner said, 'Gentlemen, welcome to Kanchipuram.'

After everyone had said their thanks, he continued. 'We have already circulated the picture of the suspect to all the police stations. Where would you like to start first?'

David replied, 'Sir, there are two police stations in the coverage of the tower our suspect's phone is connected to. That's where we want to start.'

'Good. We are here to assist you. Best wishes!'

With that, the meeting was over, and David and his team rushed to the target police stations, a Tamil Nadu police escort jeep leading their way.

By the time they stopped at the first police station, it was 8 p.m., and the inspector was just leaving. Seeing the visitors, he stopped.

David said, 'Good evening, sir. This is our suspect.'

The inspector peered at the printout and then switched on his mobile. Within seconds, he was comparing the picture in front of him with that on his phone, which Jamaluddin's friend had shared with him. Then he called out to someone, and a constable appeared.

'Get me that photo we received over email from the commissioner's office in the morning.'

The constable was back in a few seconds with another printout. This was exactly what David had with him.

He smiled and said, 'I know where the suspect is, sir.'

'Are you sure?' David asked, immediately embarrassed by his silly question.

'Yes.'

Then the inspector called Jamaluddin's friend. The phone was picked up in two rings. 'He's there now?'

'Yes, sir,' came the reply.

After disconnecting the call saying, 'Yes, sir,' Jamaluddin's friend pocketed his phone. He was sitting on the mattress while Jamaluddin was squatting on the floor.

Jamaluddin looked at him. 'Whom did you say "yes, sir" to?'

His friend hesitated before speaking. 'It was my boss. He said he wants me to come half an hour early tomorrow.'

Jamaluddin kept his eyes on his friend. His friend stammered as he continued, 'Why are you staring at me like that? Everything is okay.'

Jamaluddin leapt on him, and the two rolled on the floor as they struggled. Jamaluddin finally ended up on top and started to hit his friend. Within just a minute, there was blood all over

CASE #3 : BACK AGAINST THE WALL

the face of his friend, who was physically a lot weaker than Jamaluddin.

Jamaluddin's eyes were red with rage now, and his lips quivered as he said, 'Bastard, you informed the police about me, didn't you?'

He feebly answered, 'Why should I inform the police? And about what? What have you done, Jamal?'

There was a knock on the door. Jamaluddin jumped to his feet and reached for his bag. From it, he pulled out a knife. His friend's eyes widened, and he started to shiver.

There was another knock. This time, it was followed by an announcement: 'This is the police, Jamaluddin. Come out or we will break the door.'

Jamaluddin pulled his friend by the hair and dragged him close to the door. Then, placing the knife against his neck, he spoke through clenched teeth. 'Open the door only slightly and don't say a word.'

The friend unlatched and opened the door. There were four cops outside, their pistols drawn.

The police saw Jamaluddin immediately.

Inspector David spoke. 'Don't make it more complicated, Jamaluddin. Leave him alone.'

'No. First tell me what I have done. Why are you here?'

'You know what you have done, Jamaluddin. Give up now or we will shoot you.'

Jamaluddin gave this some thought and then said, 'Whatever you are thinking is not true. You have no proof.'

'Then what are you scared of? Drop your knife.'

Jamaluddin slowly removed the knife from the neck of his friend. Then he dropped it next to him.

David smiled. 'Nair, handcuff him.'

Jamaluddin was taken to Kochi. David and his team started to prepare a watertight case. They had all the scientific backing needed, from DNA matching to IMEI tracking.

Jaya's friends continued with their #JusticeforJaya campaign, keeping the pressure on and not letting the new government settle in. In the meantime, Jaya's father passed away one day, sad and lonely.

Finally, the case was heard in the Ernakulam sessions court a few months later. Jamaluddin looked slimmer, but he showed no remorse. After the arguments and counterarguments were completed by the prosecution and defence teams, the judge found him guilty, and he was sentenced to death by hanging.

CASE #4

RAISE THE BAR

Case overview and tools of investigation: An informer was successfully used to bait a rape accused from Nepal without formal extradition.

Location: Delhi and Nepal

Savitri Devi rushed towards the government school in Central Delhi's Daryaganj. A skinny, middle-aged woman, she was on her way to collect her only daughter, six-year-old Rohini. She checked her cheap mobile phone for the time. It was two, but the school was still a good fifteen-minutes away.

As she increased her pace, now almost running, her phone began to ring. It was her husband, Suresh.

'Have you picked her up?'

'I'm only five minutes away,' she lied, aware that her husband would get angry.

'What? It's already past two and you are still five minutes away. How many times have I told you to leave on time. It is so unsafe nowadays—'

'I know, I know,' she interrupted him.

He hung up and, knowing that her husband was right, she began to run. But as the school gate appeared in the distance, she slowed down, catching her breath. There were a lot of children right outside the gate, jostling with the elders who had come to pick them up. There were parents, elder brothers and sisters, and drivers. She knew Rohini would be waiting for her somewhere in this whirling sea of children and adults.

With her breath now in control, having realized that she was not really *that* late, she began to search for her daughter, calling her name: 'Rohini! Rohini?'

Rohini didn't respond to her calls. But this was not alarming, as Rohini was a shy girl and she might have been sitting in a quiet corner. Ten minutes later, when most of the children and those who had come to pick them up had left, and there was still no sign of Rohini, her heartbeat started to increase once again.

'Rohini? Rohini?' She paced in the vicinity of the school's gate.

'Hello, madam, what happened?' It was the guard, a youngish man in his late thirties with a large paunch and greying temples.

'My daughter … Rohini. I'm not able to find her.'

'Not able to find her?' He looked at her from top to bottom, as if trying to see if the child was hiding in her clothes. A shadow of concern passed his face.

'Rohini is in the first standard. Have you seen her?'

'Why don't you ask the class teacher? Which section is she in … Rohini?'

'One D.'

He opened the gate. 'Pannu madam is her class teacher. Madam is inside. You go and speak to her.'

Savitri Devi rushed into the school premises without thanking him. Her mind was full of questions. Rohini couldn't be inside. Her hunch was that she had just wandered off because her mother was late. But this was not possible, as her class teacher wouldn't have allowed her to. That was the rule. Only parents, or siblings, or people the child could identify were allowed to take their children home. Her husband was at work. She had reached late. Rohini had no siblings, as she was their only child. And no one Savitri Devi could think of had any business to have picked her up. These thoughts crossed her mind as she took the passageway through the lawn towards the main building of the Delhi government's school.

As soon as she entered the main corridor, she found Ms Pannu emerging from the staff room.

'Rohini's mother? How are you?' Ms Pannu, a woman in her forties, who was wearing a crisp cotton saree, had identified her.

'Where's Rohini?' a very worried-looking Savitri Devi said in reply.

'What do you mean? She left with her grandfather.'

'Left with her grandfather? Her grandfather is not here in Delhi.'

'But … ' She paused, her hand flying to her head to rake through her short hair as she took a few moments to recall. 'Her grandfather was here and Rohini had recognized him and said "Dada".'

Savitri Devi's worst nightmare had come true. Some imposter had abducted her sweet little daughter. But why? Why would anyone do that? They had no money and no enemies. Her husband worked as a salesman at a shop in Connaught Place and had no bad habits like drinking or gambling.

She felt her head spin and her body began to sway as thoughts of what her daughter might be going through at this very moment began to swim in her mind. Before she passed out, Ms Pannu stepped forward to support her, and a peon who was passing pulled a chair from a room and made her sit down.

Within a few seconds, as soon as the weakness passed, Savitri Devi was back on her feet, her fingers dialling her husband's number simultaneously. By now a few more teachers, who were yet to leave, had gathered around them.

'Come to the school fast. Someone has taken our Rohini with him.'

Suresh, her husband, was there in fifteen minutes. By now, two policemen had arrived too. Ms Pannu had informed the principal, who had in turn called 100.

'Sir, please save my daughter. Please, sir.' Suresh had tears in his eyes. He stood with his hands folded in front of the two policemen.

Savitri Devi, who had never seen her husband cry in the ten years of their married life, stood shaken, her face ashen and her eyes unblinking.

The two policemen were trying to assess the situation. The elder of the two, a man in his fifties, was inspector Ravi Kumar. He was fit for his age, and his voice was deep and raspy like that of a smoker's. The other policeman was a head constable, a skinny man in his late twenties who had the receding hairline of a man at least two decades older. His name was Pooran Bisht.

'Savitri Devi and Suresh, please come with us.' It was Ravi Kumar who spoke, his voice calm as his hand directed them towards a classroom right next to where they stood.

Before doing this, they had asked everyone except Ms Pannu and the principal to go home. The principal and Ms Pannu now sat waiting in the principal's room that was at the end of the corridor.

'Tell us about your daughter,' Ravi Kumar started.

Pooran stood a few steps behind him and was looking at the father and mother with so much intensity that his gaze seemed to be piercing right through them.

Suresh swiped his phone's screen on and showed them pictures of his daughter. Unlike his wife, he had a smart phone, and looking at the number of photos he had clicked of his daughter, he was clearly very fond of her.

'Sir, our Rohini is very beautiful, as you can see. She is also good at studies.'

'Is there anyone she calls *Dada*?'

Suresh and Savitri looked at each other before Suresh's eyes lit up and he said, 'Yes, she sometimes calls Ajay Kumar Dholi Dada.'

Savitri turned to look at him and nodded slowly, as if she was trying to recall too. 'Yes'—that was all she said.

'Ajay Kumar Dholi?'

'Yes, he's my friend,' said Suresh, before adding, 'Not really a friend, but he lives in a house not far from where we live.'

'Does he work where you work?'

'No. He works at an export factory. He's a tailor. That's what he told me.'

'Where are you from? Is he from your village?'

'Sir, we are from Bihar. He's a Nepali.'

'Then how come he's your friend?'

Suresh turned to look at his wife. A silent exchange passed between them. 'Sir, I used to borrow money from him sometimes.'

'Why? Do you drink? Drugs? GB Road?'

'No, sir,' Suresh replied in a louder voice, standing up. Then, with a finger raised at Inspector Ravi, he shouted, 'What are you talking about? I've had enough of this. You might be the police, but we are not thieves or some characterless people.'

Ravi looked at him calmly. He gave Suresh's reaction some thought. Then he smiled and said, 'Keep your head cool. We will do everything we can to get your daughter back.'

Suresh sat down, placed his face in his hands and began to sob. His wife placed her head on her husband's shoulder and began to cry too.

Twenty kilometres north of the school, Ajay Kumar Dholi got out of the autorickshaw. Rohini was holding his index finger. She looked up and smiled at him. As he smiled back, she clutched his finger tightly and said, 'Dada.'

Ajay was seething with anger. He tugged at her, and the two started to walk into the densely wooded area that was right in front of them. It was an October afternoon. The day was hot but not hot enough for anyone to complain. He knew clearly what he had to do. As they walked, he took his phone out and switched it off.

Ajay had prepared well. He had already resigned from his job, where he worked as a tailor alongside two hundred other tailors in a Noida basement, collected his final payment and packed all his items into two neat bundles at his home.

Now was the exciting part. In anticipation of this moment, he had laid awake in bed for weeks. Even though he had a solid reason to do what he was about to do, at this moment, everything except for what lay ahead had vanished from his mind.

After they had walked for about a hundred metres and he was sure the girl's screams wouldn't be heard by anyone, he stopped. The girl looked at him, took the final bite of the chocolate he had given her and smiled. 'Dada, where's Mummy?'

There was a mild edge to her voice. He knew now there was no time to lose. He lowered himself to one knee, and when his eyes were at the same level as the girl's, he smiled.

'Mummy?' The girl looked around.

Without a word, Ajay started to undress her. The girl cooperated. She had no idea what was in store for her. Once she was naked, it was his turn.

Half an hour and hundreds of screams later, Ajay zipped his pants up and, leaving behind a six-year-old in a pool of blood, began to walk back towards the road. His face was flushed and he was smiling.

Back at the school, the two policemen had got all the information they wanted. Even though it appeared to Suresh that they were working slowly, the police had been taking all steps in the quickest possible time and were constantly in touch with the control room. Therefore, by now they had the telephone number of the suspect and were on their way to the place where the phone's location was last detected. Before they left, they had asked Suresh and his wife to go home.

Half an hour later, when the police jeep pulled up at the last known position of the suspect's phone, all they could see was a deserted road that had a jungle on one side of it. Acting on a hunch, both disembarked and started to walk into the jungle. They had drawn their 9mm pistols, and their faces were taut in concentration. It took them just half an hour to spot Rohini. She was naked and lying upside down.

It did not look good. There was just too much blood around her. Ravi clicked two pictures in less than three seconds, bent down and reached for her nose to check if she was breathing. He wasn't sure. He checked for a pulse and thought he felt a faint sensation. As he was doing this, his partner explored the area to look for the perpetrator or any clues. There was no sign of the suspect.

Pooran called up the control room and relayed the information.

'Sir, the ambulance will reach in fifteen minutes,' he informed Inspector Ravi as soon as he hung up.

'We can't wait.' Saying this, Ravi lifted the girl, wrapped her clothes, which lay next to her, around her and started to move towards the jeep. Pooran followed right behind.

'No,' Ravi said loudly without turning back. 'You stay put here. Don't touch anything; let the lab team collect all the evidence. We have to catch this bastard.'

The nearest hospital was two kilometres away. As he drove, he called Suresh and asked him to come to the hospital, saying his daughter was found but that she was badly injured.

The doctor in the emergency ward where the inspector brought Rohini declared her 'brought dead'. When Suresh and Savitri Devi arrived and got the news moments later, they were devastated.

The rape of a minor is the most heinous of crimes, and the Delhi police decided to accord top priority to the case. As soon as Pooran arrived at the hospital, therefore, he and Inspector Ravi departed for the ISBT bus stop, where someone had spotted a similar-looking man.

On their way, Inspector Ravi's phone rang. It was DCP (crime) Delhi central. 'Ravi, this man should be caught.'

'Right, sir. A lookalike has been spotted at the bus stop. We are on our way. The suspect's picture has been circulated at the airport terminals, railway stations and all bus stations. Roadblocks have also been erected.'

Over the next week, the police kept a sharp lookout on all the exit routes, but the suspect was not sighted. Ravi had also positioned two constables right across the suspect's house, so that if the suspect visited his house even briefly, he could be apprehended. But all their efforts failed.

After one week, Ravi and Pooran reached the suspect's house and broke the main door lock. By now, they had obtained a search warrant.

It was a one-room house with a tiny kitchen and a closet-sized bathroom. There were no belongings except a few cardboard boxes, a rotten takeaway paper box and a few discarded old clothes. The police photographer was called, and after the area was extensively photographed, the evidence was collected in bags and their details recorded.

Since the day of the tragic rape and murder of Rohini, her mother and father remained outside the police station from morning to late at night. Although Inspector Ravi spoke to them sometimes, he avoided doing this, because in his line of work, there was no room for emotions. He was investigating the brutal rape and murder of a minor, and there were established procedures to follow.

After the police had collected the evidence from the home of the suspect and the crime scene, the next step was obvious—matching the DNA, so that suspect could be pinned down to the crime.

'Sir, I think we should send these for DNA analysis,' Pooran suggested.

'I've been thinking about the same thing. But Pooran, tell me, where do you think he has vanished? Is he really hiding in Delhi?'

'Sir, my gut instinct says he left Delhi soon after the crime. Perhaps an hour or two before we sent the lookout notice and erected roadblocks.'

Although Inspector Ravi shared the same thought, he wanted to understand Pooran's logic. After all, as a senior, it was also his responsibility to train Pooran on the job.

'Perhaps you are right. But why do you think so?'

'Sir, his house … It's empty. He has been planning this for weeks. The bastard.' Pooran banged the table hard.

'Hey, cool down. How many times do I have to tell you that a good policeman is the one who knows how to control his nerves.'

'Sorry, sir. But we must get the bastard.'

'We must get the *suspect*, not the *bastard*.'

Pooran inhaled deeply and nodded.

Inspector Ravi began, his deep voice almost a slow rumble. 'So there are three possibilities. One, he's hiding somewhere in Delhi. Two, he's escaped Delhi before our roadblocks were set up and he could now be anywhere in India. Three, he's escaped to his native Nepal.'

'In Delhi, he will be caught sooner or later, sir. But the second and third are problem areas.'

'Let's begin with Nepal.' Inspector Ravi picked up a file and read out an address. 'All rapists are cowards, and all cowards know only one thing ... to run. Run as far as possible and as fast as possible.'

The Delhi police sanctioned a three-day trip to Nepal, and the two-member team of Inspector Ravi and Head Constable Pooran Bisht left for Kathmandu immediately.

When Inspector Ravi and Head Constable Pooran landed in Nepal, they knew there were two main problems to be sorted out. The first one was bigger—was the suspect there? The second one was procedural—how much time would the bureaucracy take to honour the extradition treaty that India and Nepal had entered into back in 1953? In the extradition treaty, even though rape and murder were explicitly mentioned under Article 3, they were under no illusion that the judicial and bureaucratic procedures would be easy to deal with.

Right after landing at the Kathmandu airport, they met Inspector Milan Thapa, their appointed liaison from the Nepal police. Thapa was around five feet six inches tall, of medium build and had a sparse moustache that hung half an inch from both edges of his constantly smiling mouth. Just like the two police officers he had come to meet, Inspector Thapa was in plain clothes.

It was mid-November by now, and there was a chill in the air as they started moving in a hired taxi towards Nalang, a small town of around ten thousand inhabitants.

'How much time will it take?' Inspector Ravi asked as soon as they started. Although he knew that their destination was three hours away, he asked to initiate the conversation.

'It's three hours.' Saying this, Thapa tried to curl the sides of his moustache in an effort to make them stand up, but as soon as he moved his hands away, they fell to the sides just like before. Inspector Ravi noticed this and smiled.

'We will stop for dinner on the way. If we take twenty minutes there, we can reach the target's location by 9.20 p.m.'

Ravi looked at his wristwatch. The time was 6 p.m. In the front seat, Pooran looked ahead, not keen on talking. The taxi moved silently on an almost empty road, dense trees passing them on both sides.

After dinner, as soon as they started to move, Inspector Thapa said, 'Sir, my team is stationed minutes away from the location. We will barge in and see. I don't think the suspect is armed and, therefore, I don't expect any retaliation.'

'Guns?'

Thapa reached into his satchel and pulled out two pistols. He extended one towards Ravi. As soon as Ravi took it, he tapped the shoulder of Pooran from behind using the butt of the pistol.

them. In less than twenty-four hours, they received a report. The suspect had been tracked.

Inspector Ravi and Head Constable Pooran Bisht had a meeting.

'Sir, this is a jackpot. Let's start preparing a watertight case for extradition. We have all the proof, including the DNA,' Pooran said.

'Hmmm ... but what if the Nepal government refuses to admit our evidence?'

'But, sir—'

'Look, I have no clue about the intricacies of the Nepalese law, and while I, am no one to doubt its efficiency and integrity, I have neither the time nor the inclination to start reading Nepalese law books.'

'Sir, can't we depend on their prosecution team. We have so much evidence ... It's an open-and-shut case.'

'Right, Pooran, but you are not seeing my point. What if the prosecution slips up? We will be here in Delhi. Okay, even if we are allowed to travel to Nepal, we won't be allowed to speak in court about this, I am sure.'

'So?'

'There has to be a better way. We know where that bastard is.'

The two men in khaki were quiet for a few minutes. The time was 7 p.m., and night had fallen as they continued deliberating.

'Sir, I have got an idea!' Saying this, Pooran jumped to his feet.

'Sit down!' barked Inspector Ravi before he smiled. 'Hey, why do you get so hyper? Learn to keep your emotions under check.'

He sat down and said, 'Sir, our suspect is a coward and a mean son of a bitch, right?'

'Right.'

Pooran leaned forward. 'Sir, let's bait him and get him here to Delhi.'

'Tell me more.' Inspector Ravi leaned forward to listen. Now there was just a foot's distance between their faces. Their eyes locked, and for a few seconds, a silent exchange passed between them.

Pooran continued, 'Let's bait him. Create a situation ... I don't know how, but get him here to Delhi.'

'Hmm ...' Inspector Ravi said, contemplating what he had just heard. He leaned back in his chair.

Pooran got up again, and as Ravi raised his eyebrows without saying a word, Pooran said, 'Sir, let me get some tea.'

While Pooran was away, Inspector Ravi considered this option. *Is there a way that will ensure that the suspect comes to Delhi without involving the two governments?*

Five minutes later, as Pooran slid a cup of steaming tea across to his boss and settled into the opposite chair, sipping the one he held in his hand, he noticed that Inspector Ravi was smiling. He smiled too. Now all he had to do was wait.

Two minutes later, Inspector Ravi finished his tea and, placing the cup down, began to speak. 'You have used the perfect word, Pooran. Bait! Let's do something that makes our suspect believe that the case is closed and no one is looking for him. That will make him confident. Once that is achieved, let's send him a fake job offer, with a salary that's at least four times what he is earning in Nepal.'

'Right, sir. The kind of person he is, greedy and selfish, this shouldn't be hard if we take precautions.'

'Precautions, right.' Inspector Ravi's smile dimmed a little. 'I guess we will have to use our friend Milan Thapa here.'

'But, sir—'

'No, wait. What's your opinion of the Nepali inspector?'

'Sir, to me he appeared professional.'

'I would use the word *practical*. And *practical* is better than *professional*. I have been in the police force for thirty years now, Pooran, and whenever I look someone in the eyes, nine times out of ten, I can read their exact intentions.'

'And?'

'I think we can depend on him. In any case, we don't have any other choice. The Delhi police will not send us hunting for a cold case suspect in Nepal during this festive period.'

Inspector Ravi called Inspector Milan Thapa of the Nepal police, and their conversation lasted only ten minutes. By now, it was close to nine, and Ravi's wife had called him thrice, but he was unable to take her calls.

He looked at Pooran, and as soon as he opened his mouth to say something, his phone rang again. It was his wife. He sent her a message saying 'I will call you back' and started: 'Milan has assured me that he will cooperate. Now, we need to take a few actions.' He went on to tell Pooran exactly what was needed.

By the time Inspector Ravi and Pooran left for their homes, it was almost midnight. Promising to think it over that night, Ravi had asked Pooran to reach the office by seven the next morning. Right outside the police station, both went their own ways: Inspector Ravi turned left, towards the police quarters ten kilometres away, and Pooran right, towards his parents' home.

By afternoon the next day, the entire operation was finalized. There were three stages. In stage one, Inspector Milan Thapa was to find someone who would act as an informer. In stage two, this informer would convince the suspect that the case in Delhi was closed. After this, the suspect would be given a job offer through the informer. In stage three, the suspect, assuming that he took the bait, would be arrested in Delhi as soon as he arrived in the capital for the lucrative job.

Around one thousand kilometres away in Nepal, a few days later, the operation was kicked into action.

One evening, as Ajay Kumar Dholi left the shop in Nalang where he worked as a tailor for a measly sum of ten thousand rupees per month, his friend Laxman Bahadur met up with him.

'Arre, Laxman. *Tapaaii lai kasto cha?* (How are you?)'

'*Malaai sanchai cha* (I'm fine).' Laxman slapped Dholi's back as the two walked.

Laxman and Dholi had been friends ever since Laxman had come to live next door to Dholi around the same time Dholi had returned from Delhi. Laxman had no idea why Dholi had left his job in Delhi where he was paid so well. On being asked, Dholi had said that his boss was a bastard and had falsely implicated him in a police case and he had no option but to leave India. The two used to meet off and on.

When they neared their houses, Laxman said, 'Come to my house. I have got good whisky.'

Dholi's eyes brightened but only for a second. 'Whisky? Last week you said you had no money.'

'I will tell you all about that when we start drinking.'

The two of them bent down to get inside through the low door. Just like Dholi, Laxman lived alone. He flicked a light switch on and a naked bulb blinded them for a second with its bright light. In the small room, there was a cot on one side and two plastic chairs separated by a teapoy were placed in the centre.

Dholi collapsed into one of the chairs and said, 'Whisky.'

Laxman reached inside the bag that he had been carrying all along and pulled out a Johnnie Walker whisky bottle.

'Red Label!' he announced and placed it with a flourish on the teapoy.

'Oh my God!' Dholi picked it up and felt the cold glass of the bottle by placing it on his cheek, his eyes closing simultaneously. 'I have never had this—only seen it in the movies. Where did you get this from?'

'I snatched the bag of a gora.'

Dholi gave him a long look. 'Hmm ... and what else did you find inside?'

'Clothes, mostly, all large-sized, so I threw them outside on the road. There was no money.'

'You never told me you like to steal.'

'How about you?'

'I am just a tailor,' Dholi lamented with a tinge of resignation.

Laxman got two steel glasses and poured two large pegs, mixed water into the glasses and extended a glass towards Dholi. 'Cheers!'

Dholi had no idea that Laxman was putting into action a carefully planned operation of the Nepal police. An inspector called Milan Thapa had met him the previous day and explained everything about Dholi and the fact that he was a monster who had raped and murdered a child and was now hiding in Nepal. An upright and hardworking man, Laxman was furious. The man he had thought to be an innocent fellow countryman was, in fact, a wanted criminal. He had, therefore, agreed to help the Nepal police. Inspector Thapa had offered him a reward on the successful completion of this mission, but he had politely declined.

In one hour, half of the whisky bottle that Inspector Thapa had given to Laxman was gone, and the two men were now laughing and high-fiving each other for almost everything, however silly. Laxman had been careful and was drinking far less than Dholi. Another hour later, by the time Dholi left, the bottle was nearly three-fourths finished and the two had eaten a quickly fixed meal of bread and eggs that Laxman had prepared on the small stove in the room.

It took Laxman three such drinking sessions to make Dholi take the bait.

After the expensive Scotch whisky had run out, Laxman had offered local rum so as not to raise suspicion. They had become thick friends by now.

One morning, Laxman, who had been waiting, left his house when he spotted Dholi leaving his house.

'Late today?' Dholi remarked, patting Laxman's back as the two started to move towards the main road.

'Yes, was feeling a little low this morning.'

'Hmm …'

'Brother, listen, remember I promised you that I would check the status of your case with my friend who works in the Delhi police?'

Dholi stiffened a bit and had only a hazy recollection of the moment he had said this during one of their binge-drinking sessions. 'Yes, what about it?'

'Well, he called and said your case has been closed permanently.'

Dholi eased up a little as they walked for a few minutes before Laxman played the final card. 'Another thing: I have a friend in Noida. He says there is a vacancy for a tailor there. They will give forty thousand'—he paused for a second or two before continuing—' but one has to work for twelve hours, no holidays ...'

By now, Laxman and Dholi had reached the bus stop. As Dholi took a bus that arrived just then, Laxman continued to walk towards his place of work that was only a kilometre away.

He reported the progress to Inspector Milan Thapa. Now, he was told, all they had to do was wait. The same evening, as Laxman was preparing food in his house, there was a knock. It was 8 p.m. When he opened the door, he was surprised to see Dholi standing there holding a bottle of whisky in his hand. It was Johnnie Walker Red Label.

'What? Did you steal from a gora too?' He stepped aside to allow a very happy-looking Dholi to get in.

'No, I bought it with my money.'

They started to drink. After a few minutes of small talk, Dholi got to business. 'About that job you mentioned. Can you connect me to your friend?'

'Sure.' Laxman had expected this and called a number from his phone. 'Hey, Bibek. You told me about that job, remember, that tailor job in Noida?'

On the other end was Inspector Ravi. 'Yes, the company's name is Kishan Fabrics. Note down the number: 9910116453. Noted?'

Laxman grabbed a pen and paper and wrote it down. 'Noted.'

'This is the supervisor's number. His name is Gagan Kumar. Speak to him.'

Laxman disconnected and looked at Dholi. 'Call this number.'

Dholi kept the glass on the teapoy and dialled from his mobile, unaware that he was about to speak to an expert interpreter from the Delhi police. The call lasted five minutes. After disconnecting, he looked at Laxman and smiled. 'Thank you. You are right. They are giving me forty thousand. I will leave as soon as I can.'

'Congratulations.' Laxman smiled. 'Happy to help. You now have the number of the supervisor, so call him whenever you want. But please don't forget me after you go to Delhi and start living the high life.'

Dholi gave him a half smile and said, 'I'm an honest man. I will never forget this favour.'

Dholi had no idea what was in store for him, and he certainly wouldn't forget Laxman ever.

After a month, when Dholi shared his arrival plan with the supervisor, the supervisor asked him to go straight to a small hotel in Daryaganj near New Delhi railway station.

On a chilly December morning, a confident-looking Ajay Kumar Dholi arrived at the hotel. He checked in at the reception and took the keys to his room, which was on the second floor. When he opened the room, he had whisky on his mind, as his job was to start from the next day.

He inhaled deeply and pushed open the door, his smile now the widest it had been. The room was dark, and he slipped the plastic key card into the slot next to the door. The lights turned on and he saw two people he would never have imagined seeing, not even in his wildest dreams—his friend Suresh and Suresh's wife, Savitri Devi.

It took him a few seconds to grasp the situation, and he turned on his heels. As soon as he did, he came face to face with two men in khaki. Their badges read: 'Ravi Kumar' and 'Pooran Bisht.'

Inspector Ravi nodded at Suresh, who stepped forward and slapped Dholi, as Savitri Devi broke down inconsolably on seeing the man who had raped and killed their daughter.

Handcuffed by Pooran, Dholi was taken away. Just before leaving, Inspector Ravi looked at Suresh and Savitri Devi and said, 'The Delhi police will do everything in its capacity to make sure that this bastard is hanged.'

During interrogation, Ajay Kumar Dholi revealed that he had raped Suresh's daughter because he wanted to teach him a lesson. On being asked why, he said that even though he had helped Suresh tide over his financial difficulties many times, Suresh used to swear at him and he didn't like being sworn at.

CASE #5

SKELETON IN THE CLOSET

Case overview and tools of investigation: The narco-analysis test was used to crack an eight-year-old murder case involving the victim's wife and her paramour.

Location: Delhi, Rewari (Haryana) and Alwar (Rajasthan)

The spring of 2010 was beautiful. It was particularly special for Saraswati, a young woman in her early twenties who lived in a village called Gelpur, because she had fallen in love for the first time in her life.

The man who had won her heart was Karan Singhal, a businessman who supplied building materials to the rapidly urbanizing area around the village, which was located on the border of Rajasthan and Haryana, at a distance of just under two hours from Delhi.

The two lovers had been meeting secretly in small parks and isolated corners, holding hands, kissing and vowing to remain by each other's side for the rest of their lives. But there was a problem. In fact, a big problem—they belonged to different castes. Therefore, as soon as Saraswati's parents found out about the affair, they finalized her marriage to a tempo driver named Ravi Kumar who lived in Rajokri in Delhi.

After fixing the marriage, her parents locked a heartbroken Saraswati in the house. Karan was furious, but he didn't know what to do.

After a few days, one afternoon, taking advantage of the post-lunch lull in her house, Saraswati packed a small bag and escaped. She went straight to Karan's warehouse, looked into his eyes and said, 'I have left my house for you. Let's run away to another place.'

He embraced her and said, 'I love you, Saraswati. But we can't run away like this.'

She pushed him away, tears in her eyes and said, 'Why not? All we need to do is take a taxi and elope. Before anyone comes to know, we will be in Delhi.'

Karan tried to make her sit down on a stool, but she kept standing, her face turned away from him. He inhaled deeply and tried to explain. 'This is not the way, darling. The police will catch us sooner or later. And my business is here in Gelpur. What will I do in Delhi? How will I support us?'

Saraswati began to sob, her bag by her side and her plan rejected.

Karan continued, 'We need to take every step carefully, darling.'

She looked at him, her eyes hopeful once again. 'What do you think we should do?'

'You get married to that ... whatever his name is. But after the wedding, don't have physical relations with him. I will attend the wedding too. The very next day, you come back to Gelpur. I would have worked it out by then.'

Saraswati continued staring at him without a word, her brain trying to process what her lover had just said. Karan added, 'Trust me, darling. We will be together soon after that. I want to play it smart ... save my business and have you in my house as my wife soon.'

She finally smiled and repeated after him, 'Wife, yes. I want to be *your* wife.'

He pulled her close and gave her a deep kiss. After a few minutes, Saraswati returned to her house with her bag. No one had noticed anything.

For the next few months, Saraswati and Karan could meet only occasionally, but whenever they did, he assured her that he was close to coming up with a foolproof plan. In his spare time, Karan watched crime movies and did extensive online research on how to conduct a perfect murder. One of the movies he watched several times was *Humraaz*, loosely based on the English movie *A Perfect Murder*.

One morning in January 2011, taking advantage of the winter fog, Saraswati went to visit Karan one last time. It was a passionate meeting. After they overcame their emotions, Karan shared his plan with her.

He held her by the shoulders and said, 'Listen carefully, Saraswati. The pheras will get over at around two or three in the morning. After that, you leave with that man for Rajokri. It will take you two and a half hours to reach, so it will be five or six in the morning. Clear, so far?'

She nodded.

Karan kissed her gently and continued, 'As per custom, you know you will have to come back that day. Try to leave as soon as you can. Once you are here, I will tell you the next step.'

She was beginning to get irritated. 'Next step? What will you do? How will you get me out of this marriage and how will *we* get married? I'm not sure this is a good plan. I think I should not get married. You take me now. Let's elope.'

Karan shook his head. 'Darling, why don't you understand? My money is invested here. People owe me money in the market. If we elope, I can't come back and we will be penniless. What sort of life will we have if we have no money?'

'But—'

He raised his hand to stop her and said, 'I'll kill him. It will be the perfect crime. No one will ever find out. Once he is dead, you can come back here. You will be a widow and no one will marry you. After that, I will ask your father for your hand in marriage and I am sure he will agree. I will also give him some money.'

She smiled and relaxed; that she had just agreed to kill another man didn't occur to her. All she was thinking about was her union with her paramour.

Finally, on 8 February 2011, dressed in her bridal finery, Saraswati waited for her baraat to arrive. Her parents had made modest arrangements, and the groom's family seemed happy. There was a lot of dancing and cheering. Firecrackers were burst and there was an atmosphere of merriment. Her parents were ecstatic. She was, after all, getting married to a man from Delhi, someone who earned twenty thousand rupees as a tempo driver.

Karan was present at the wedding function. He was sad, but he smiled and didn't let his made-up expression slip. Those who knew about Saraswati and Karan's affair felt sorry for them but were also relieved at the maturity of the two of them in giving in to the demands of the culture and upholding the wishes of their elders.

In the end, at around 3 a.m., Saraswati left along with the groom's entourage, seated beside her husband. Ravi tried to strike up a conversation with Saraswati but she didn't say a single word during the entire journey. Once, he placed his hand on her hand and whispered, 'I know you are sad, my wife, but I promise to take care of you and love you with all my heart.'

In response, she pulled her hand away. The car continued to make its way towards Rajokri.

It was almost six when they arrived at Ravi's house in Rajokri. There were a few relatives waiting to greet the new bride, and after a few customs, Saraswati was escorted to a room. Women, old and young, and a few in their teens, surrounded her and showered her with praises.

But she was suffocating on the inside, and her ears were waiting for the familiar honk of Karan's car. She knew that her father had agreed to Karan's proposal to use his car and driver to bring her back to Gelpur for the customary return trip.

At one in the afternoon, her heart skipped a beat as she heard the familiar horn. Finally, her head covered and eyes downcast, she smiled.

Minutes later, she was escorted to the main door, where her husband, Ravi, was waiting for her. He saw her smiling as their eyes met for the briefest of moments. Then she got inside the car.

Ravi bent down and whispered, 'I'll miss you. Please come back soon.'

She didn't respond. The car started to drive away.

The car was being driven by Rajesh, Karan's driver. He looked at her in the rearview mirror and smiled.

She smiled at him and asked, 'How's Karan?'

'He will be fine once you are back in Gelpur.'

She laughed. The trouble was over for her, at least temporarily, and she knew she could trust Karan to come up with a good plan to kill Ravi.

For the next few weeks, Karan didn't meet Saraswati or even go close to her house. Meanwhile, at her house, her parents grew more worried with each passing day as she refused to go back to Ravi's house.

Her mother asked her, 'What's wrong? You are married now. You have to go back to your sasural. They have been calling us every day.'

'Mom, I want to be with you for some more days. What's the hurry?'

'Don't be a child. You are a married woman now.'

'Mom, I agree. Just a few more days and I promise I will leave.'

Saraswati had been very worried since her arrival. There had been no word from Karan. As she was contemplating her next move, one day she received a note from him. She opened the crumpled paper, her heart beating wildly.

You go back to Delhi. Don't have physical relations with that man. Tell him you two should spend some time together. first. The next day, convince him to take you for a visit to your cousin sister's place, followed by a movie. I will meet you two on the way. After that, you leave it to me. Love you, my sweetheart.

Burn this after reading it.

She burned it immediately. Although she knew she would be free soon, she was now worried because she would have to spend one night alone with her husband in the bedroom.

'What if he rapes me?' she murmured to herself.

Her face hardened. 'I will scream for help.'

But would anyone come and break down the bedroom door? The answer was *no*. She knew she would have to be very careful.

On 21 March 2011, Saraswati returned to her husband's home. She kept her behaviour normal and spoke to everyone with a smile. Finally, as night fell, she went to the bedroom. The room had been decorated with flowers, and there were rose petals scattered on the bed. This was her wedding night. Her confidence nosedived. What if Ravi paid no attention to her pleas and raped her …

She sat on the bed and waited for Ravi to come. Finally, the door opened and she heard his footsteps. She kept her eyes down.

He walked up to the bed, hesitated and finally sat beside her. After a few moments, he said, 'Hi.'

She didn't respond to his greeting. In fact, she didn't move an inch.

'Are you annoyed with me, Saraswati?'

She didn't reply.

'I love you.'

She looked up this time, smiled and said, 'I need more time to be comfortable with you. Will you give me a few days?'

He smiled and said, 'Of course, what's the hurry? In front of the sacred fire, we have already vowed to spend our next seven lives together. What should I do? What will make you comfortable?'

This was what she was waiting for. This was her moment. She didn't miss a second. 'I want us to spend some time together, get to know each other before we ... I mean ...'

Her act was spot on. Seeing his coy wife making a request like this, Ravi picked up her hand and kissed it. Then he said, 'Yes, my love, whatever you say.'

She gently pulled her hand back but beamed in the next second as she said, 'Can we go for a movie tomorrow?'

'Yes, why not? That would be wonderful.'

'But on the way to the cinema hall, I want to visit a relative's house briefly. Just for ten minutes, if that's okay.'

'Yes, that's a good plan.'

Saraswati was relieved, but she was still not free of all the dangers. She lay down on the bed and whispered, 'Good night, darling.'

'Good night, my love.'

Ravi sat there for a few seconds and then he too lay down next to his wife. He turned to look at her. Saraswati had closed her eyes, and after lying awake for an hour, he closed his eyes too.

The next morning, Saraswati woke early, as did Ravi. By 10 a.m., they were both ready. Ravi had noticed Saraswati was smiling a lot and there was confidence in her movements. He took this as a good sign and knew that within the next few days he would consummate the marriage. He hated the idea of having to force himself on his wife. It was all going well for him, he thought.

They drove in Ravi's tempo to Saraswati's cousin's house. To help Ravi overcome any discomfort or doubts, Saraswati took the initiative of holding his hand in the moving vehicle. He smiled and squeezed her hand.

Saraswati kept her eyes on the road as they moved. The route to her cousin's house was known to Karan, and she knew he would be waiting to waylay them along the way.

After some time, when they were minutes away from her cousin's house, she saw Karan stepping in front of their vehicle, waving his hand. Ravi applied the brakes swiftly and started to shout at the stranger who had just decided to step in front of his tempo.

Saraswati turned towards him and said, 'No, it's okay.' Then she looked at Karan and, feigning surprise, she said, 'Karan ji, you?'

Karan looked as surprised and said, 'Hey, nice to see you, Saraswati ji. I'm sorry, I didn't see the vehicle coming. I was just crossing the road.'

Ravi looked at his wife and then at Karan. At that moment, he recognized Karan from the wedding.

Ravi extended his hand. 'I saw you at our wedding. How are you?'

Karan gleefully shook his hand and said, 'I'm fine.'

Meanwhile, another man who had been hovering behind Karan folded his hands to Ravi and Saraswati and greeted them. Karan turned and introduced him to Ravi. 'Have you recognized him? He is Rajesh, my driver. He had, in fact, gone to your house the day after your wedding to bring Saraswati back.'

The vehicles behind the tempo started to honk, and Ravi said, 'Can I drop you somewhere?'

Karan said, 'Yes, can we join you? You can drop us five kilometres down this road if you are going that far or up to where you are going.'

Ravi said, 'We are going two more kilometres down this road. But after I drop Saraswati off at her cousin's place, I will drop you ahead.'

Karan and Rajesh got inside as Karan said, 'Thank you very much.'

The vehicle started to move. Within minutes, they dropped Saraswati off and continued ahead. After a few hundred metres, Karan said, 'I want to buy a cigarette. Can you stop there?' He pointed to a kiosk that was ahead. Ravi braked and the vehicle stopped.

That's when Rajesh hit Ravi on the head from behind him with an iron rod. Ravi slumped in his seat. Pulling him out of the driver's seat, the two of them taped his mouth and tied both his hands and legs. Then Rajesh started driving the tempo. After ten minutes, he turned on to an isolated road, and they could now see Karan's car parked there. They got down and dragged the unconscious Ravi to the ground. Then they took him behind Karan's car and looked around. There was no one in sight.

Karan had already struck a deal with his driver, Rajesh, for seventy thousand rupees to help him kill Ravi and dispose of the body. The two of them dragged Ravi into the bushes to a place where they were satisfied that passing vehicles would not be able to spot them. Then Karan sliced a knife deep through Ravi's neck, as Rajesh kept him pinned down. Within a few minutes, Ravi was dead.

Leaving Rajesh next to the body, Karan walked back to the road, and once he was sure there was no one in sight, he went back to where Rajesh was. The two of them then dragged the body to Karan's car and dumped it in the boot.

Karan straightened and said, 'Now let me wipe away the fingerprints and you go back to the spot where we killed him and cover the blood on the ground with soil. Take the shovel from the backseat.'

Karan then took out his handkerchief and cleaned all the places in the tempo the two of them had touched. By the time he was done, Rajesh was back too, and the two of them sat in the car without a word and started to drive towards Gelpur.

After an hour, according to the plan, Saraswati called her father-in-law and informed him that Ravi had dropped her off but had not returned to pick her up. She waited for a few more hours and then returned on her own. By late evening, everyone was worried.

She heard the family members calling all their friends and relatives. She knew they would never find Ravi now. She was happy that she was finally going to be with the man who truly loved her. Her thoughts briefly turned to Ravi, and she wondered if she liked him at all. In the end, she realized she didn't.

CASE #5 : SKELETON IN THE CLOSET

By the next morning, Ravi's father had filed a missing person's report at the Kapashera police station. Since a case related to the reporting of a missing person was considered a non-cognizable offence, the police made an entry in the General Station Diary (GSD) as per procedure and initiated an inquiry.

The inquiry was assigned to Sub-Inspector Mehtab Singh Yadav and Head Constable Ram Pyara Kumar. Ravi's father had provided all the details related to his son, including his latest picture and the fact that he was last seen with his wife, Saraswati.

The two of them, therefore, started their inquiry at Ravi's residence the very next day. While Mehtab was a six-foot-two-inch-tall man in his forties, Ram Pyara was in his mid-twenties and five feet seven inches tall, just sufficient to join the Delhi police as a constable in the executive branch.

Mehtab paused in front of Ravi's door and looked around. The house was located in a narrow lane, and people stood around looking at the two men in uniform curiously. There were eyes staring at them from the windows as well. A hen ran past them just then, chased by a huge cock.

He knocked. The door was opened by a lean, middle-aged man who looked ill. They didn't have to ask him if he was the missing person's father.

He escorted the two policemen into the small room, and as soon as they sat down, he opened his mouth to speak. But he choked and began to wail instead.

Sub-Inspector Mehtab cut him short. 'Your son has been missing for only two days. He must have gone to a friend's place. He will come back. Trust me, I know these young men these days.'

Ravi's father froze for a few seconds, his brain trying to understand what was being said. Then he spoke, his voice breaking after every few words. 'Sir, no ... our Ravi is not like that. He just got married. In fact, his wife joined us just the day before he went missing.'

'What about Ravi's friends? Drinking habits?'

'He has very few friends, sir, and no one he is close to. He is a very quiet sort of boy. Never quarrels with anyone.'

Mehtab was irritated. 'Sir, please answer what I ask you. Does he drink?'

'No.'

'Cigarettes, ganja?'

'Never.'

'Gambling?'

'No.'

'Womanizing?'

Ravi's father was on his feet.

'Sit down!' roared the sub-inspector, and Ravi's father sat down, now looking frightened.

Mehtab inhaled deeply and then spoke, clearly trying his best to sound calm. 'Look, we have to ask these questions. It is not about your son; this is procedure. We have to start eliminating possibilities. Please don't mind.'

Ravi's father nodded.

'When did he get married?'

'Sir, on 8 February.'

'But you said his wife joined him just a day before he went missing. That means she joined him on ...'

'On 22 March.'

'Why so many days after the wedding?'

'Sir, she went back in the afternoon the day she arrived. In fact, she stayed here only for a few hours.'

Mehtab turned to exchange a glance with Ram Pyara.

'Why? Was she underage at the time of the marriage?'

'No, sir. She was twenty-one. She said she was missing her parents and wanted to stay with them for a few weeks.'

Mehtab was on his feet. 'Where is she?'

'In her room.'

Mehtab and Ram Pyara followed Ravi's father. He knocked on a door, and when there was no answer, he gently pushed the door open.

Saraswati was sitting on the bed, her legs folded so that her chin rested on her knees. Her eyes were moist. She wore no makeup, though her saree was covered in heavy embroidery.

Ravi's father cleared his throat and said, 'The police are here. They want to ask you a few questions.'

She didn't lift her eyes. She just nodded.

Sub-Inspector Mehtab took a step closer and noticed her body shiver. He knew from experience that initial reactions offered the best clues.

'Saraswati ji, look at me.'

She took a few moments and then lifted her head and slowly raised her eyes to meet Mehtab's. He stared at her unblinking eyes, and she did the same.

'When your husband dropped you at your cousin's house, was there anyone else in the tempo besides the two of you?'

She nodded.

Ravi's father spoke from behind in a surprised voice. 'What? Who was there? Why didn't you tell me before?'

Without turning his head, Mehtab said in a slightly raised voice, 'Sir, please don't interrupt the inquiry, or I will have to send you away.'

'Sorry, sir.' That was all Ravi's father said in a voice that now sounded low and underconfident.

Mehtab continued in a level voice, 'Yes, tell me who else was there.'

Saraswati told them that they had been on their way, when they bumped into Karan and his driver, Rajesh, and offered them a lift.

After a few more questions, Mehtab led them out of the room, leaving Saraswati alone.

At the main door, he paused and said, 'If your son comes back or anything else happens that you think is important, please call us.'

Ram Pyara dictated their phone numbers, which Ravi's father promptly saved on his phone.

After this, the two policemen climbed into their jeep and returned to the police station.

On the way, Mehtab asked, 'Ram Pyara, how many cases of missing persons have you handled so far?'

Ram Pyara smiled and said, 'Sir, more than one hundred.'

'Great! So what do you think about this one?'

'Sir, I think this woman is involved.'

'And why do you think that?'

'Sir, I have been in the police for only five years, but when I meet a criminal, I can recognize them.'

Mehtab laughed and said after a few seconds, 'Not so fast, Ram Pyara. Not so fast.'

A day earlier, after stuffing Ravi's body in the boot of the car, Karan and Rajesh had driven back to Gelpur, arriving there before four in the evening. They had parked the car next to Karan's warehouse, which was located in an isolated place outside the village and comprised three small, interconnected rooms covered by a tin shed.

After night fell, the two of them started digging adjacent to the warehouse. They worked hard for several hours. The idea was to dig a pit deep enough that the dogs couldn't pull the body out. Finally, after ten at night, they removed Ravi's body from the boot of the car and rolled it into the pit. It took them another half an hour to fill the pit, and by the time they were done, both of them were exhausted. Then they cleaned themselves up and returned to their houses.

Two days later, Karan received visitors he wasn't expecting. As he opened the door, he found three policemen standing at the threshold. He recognized the local policeman from Gelpur and realized the other two were from the Delhi police.

The tall one from the Delhi police spoke first. 'Karan Singhal?'

He nodded.

'I'm Sub-Inspector Mehtab Singh, and this is Head Constable Ram Pyara. We are here regarding a missing person called Ravi Kumar. You and your driver were last seen with the missing person and his wife.'

'Missing person? Is Saraswati's husband missing?'

'That's right. Tell us what happened after Saraswati was dropped off on 22 March.'

He squinted his eyes, trying to think, and after a few seconds said, 'Sir, he dropped Saraswati at 12.10 and after that ... around two kilometres ahead on MG Road, he dropped us too.'

'What time was that?'

'It was 12.20, sir.'

Mehtab laughed. The idea was to make Karan nervous. Then he asked, 'Do you always note the time so precisely?'

Karan answered, keeping a straight face, 'Sir, for businessmen like me, time is money. No, I don't track time like this when I am here in Gelpur, but when I travel outside, I keep a close watch on the time.'

'Good. So tell us what time you ate dinner on 22 March.'

'Sir, we had eaten a late lunch, so we didn't eat any dinner. By the time we reached Gelpur that day, everything was closed.'

As they interviewed Karan, the local constable left to bring Rajesh.

As soon as Rajesh arrived, Ram Pyara took him out of earshot and asked him the same questions.

By the time Ram Praya was back, he was smiling ear to ear.

Mehtab looked at him, smiling as widely as him, and remarked, 'Looks like my friend Ram Pyara has found a gold mine.'

Ram Pyara nodded enthusiastically, and then leaving Rajesh and Karan standing uncertainly side by side, they left in the jeep they had arrived in. They first went to the Gelpur police station to drop the local cop, and after that they left for Delhi.

As soon as they hit the highway, Mehtab asked, 'So, what have you got?'

'Sir, that bastard Karan is lying.'

'And how do you know that?'

'Because I was present when you interviewed Karan. I asked the same questions to Rajesh, and he gave me the same reply—the exact time they dropped the bride, the exact time they were dropped, the story about their late lunch and arriving here after all the shops had shut.'

'And?'

'The ultimate was when I asked him how he remembered the exact time, he said the same thing that Karan had said. "Daal mein kaala nahin, sir—yahan to saari daal hi kaali hai (It's not just a speck of black in the daal, sir—the whole daal is black)."'

'Hmm ... so it is clear now—these two men are in this together. And that woman is somehow involved too. But what we have right now is not good enough. All this is circumstantial evidence. We need proof. Solid proof.'

'Right, sir.'

'And I know getting proof needs time. Let's see what happens next.'

'This sure is an interesting case, sir.'

'All cases in which a woman doesn't like her husband or a husband doesn't like his wife become interesting sooner or later.'

'You think this woman didn't like her husband?'

'That's what my gut instinct says. And my gut is seldom wrong.'

Sub-Inspector Mehtab moved a request to his boss for a polygraph test for the three people who were last seen with the missing person: Saraswati, Karan and Rajesh. He supplemented it with his preliminary investigation report and the fact that Ravi Kumar had no enemies and no one would have had a motive to kill him.

The request was approved, and within a month of the date Ravi had gone missing, Sub-Inspector Mehtab Singh Yadav scheduled visits for his three suspects to a forensics centre in Delhi.

A polygraph machine is a device that records the body's involuntary responses to an examiner's questions in order to ascertain a person's deceptive behaviour. The test measures heart rate, blood pressure, breathing rate, skin conductivity, etc. It's a computerized test that involves asking predetermined questions to the suspect and recording changes in measurements while they answer.

But there was one problem. The police couldn't conduct polygraph tests unless the suspects agreed, thus making it a voluntary test. Therefore, after the approval was received, Mehtab and Ram Pyara drove once again to Gelpur. By now, they knew that Saraswati had moved back to her parents' house in Gelpur.

Karan invited them into his small warehouse office and said, 'Sir, can I get you chai or soft drinks?'

Mehtab wanted to ask him to shut up but chose to smile instead and said, 'Chai will be fine.'

Karan called someone on his mobile phone and ordered three cups of tea.

After he disconnected, he looked at Mehtab and Ram Pyara and smiled uncertainly.

Mehtab said in his softest voice, surprising Ram Pyara, 'See, Mr Singhal, the Delhi police are loaded with so many cases. We have no time to even breathe. As far as this Ravi's disappearance case is concerned, we want to close it fast.'

'Sir, I have already told you that I have no idea where he is.'

'I know, and I agree. But the fact is that you and your driver, Rajesh, were last seen with the man. We can't ignore these facts ...' He inhaled deeply, smiled and continued, 'I have come here to seek your help. If you cooperate with us, this case will be closed in no time. For us, it will mean one less case in our diary, and for you two, a future of not worrying about policemen knocking on your doors at odd times.'

'Sir, I'm sorry, I don't know what you need from me, but I really have no idea where he is.'

'Okay, let me put it this way—will you cooperate with me if I can make this case go away?'

'Yes, sir. I'm a law-abiding citizen. I'm ready to do anything you say.'

Mehtab leaned back in his chair and said, 'Very good.'

Just then, the door opened and a teenage boy entered the office. He was carrying three glasses of tea in a carrier made out of wire. Mehtab paused as the boy placed the glasses in front of the three men. Then the boy pulled out a packet of glucose biscuits from the pocket of his oversized trousers with the flourish of a magician and peeled the wrapper from one side.

After opening the packet, he pulled out a small paper plate from the other pocket and placed the packet of biscuits on the plate.

After the boy was gone, Karan said, *'Sir, please chai lijiye.'*

Mehtab and Ram Pyara picked up their glasses and took a sip each before setting the glasses down again.

Karan picked up the plate and, after removing the wrapper and freeing the biscuits, extended the plate towards them.

Both knew accepting his hospitality was important and, therefore, took one biscuit each.

'The chai is good,' Ram Pyara remarked.

'Sir, here in Gelpur everything is good. You must allow me to entertain you in the evening. Do you take whisky?'

Mehtab smiled to himself. This man was moving too fast.

But he remarked, 'How can the police work without whisky?'

'Right, sir.' Karan let out a short laugh, looking in full control of where this little chat was going.

But Mehtab knew they had to dig their teeth in faster. After finishing the tea, he said, 'Look, Karan, there is only one way in which we can clear your name and close this case once and for all.'

Karan's eyes brightened. 'What do I have to do, sir?'

'Appear for a polygraph test.'

'A what, sir?'

Karan knew all about polygraph tests. He had read a lot about them, but he feigned ignorance.

'Let me explain—we have a test that can catch people who are lying. Since you are speaking the truth, you don't have to worry. The machine will clear you, and this will allow us to strike your name off the list of suspects.'

CASE #5 : SKELETON IN THE CLOSET

'Sir, I am ready for any such test. What is the name once again, sir?'

'Polygraph test.' It was Ram Pyara who answered this time.

'Poly ... graph. I'm hearing the name for the first time, sir.'

Mehtab said, 'Don't worry about the name. Just answer truthfully, and the machine will clear you. I'll let you know soon when and where you have to come.'

Ram Payara took out a sheet of paper from the envelope he was carrying and extended it towards Karan. He looked at it for a few seconds and signed where he was asked to.

As Ram Pyara folded and kept the signed document back in the envelope, Mehtab asked, 'Can you call Rajesh here for his signature?'

Karan nodded and called Rajesh using his mobile phone. Rajesh was with them in less than five minutes. Ram Pyara briefly explained the polygraph test to Rajesh, who looked blankly at his boss, Karan. After Karan nodded, he signed too and left the office.

Mehtab said, 'Can you call Saraswati now?'

Karan kept a straight face and said, 'Sir, I haven't met her after that day, but I have heard that she is here at her parents' house. If you want, I can send Rajesh and ask her to come here. Or you two can go to her parents' house.'

Mehtab smiled and said, 'Send Rajesh. Thanks for making it so easy for us.'

'Sure, sir.' He called Rajesh and instructed him.

Saraswati arrived after an hour. She looked like a mare caught in the headlights of a car in the middle of the road. She heard what Ram Pyara said, nodded and signed. Mehtab noticed that she made no eye contact with Karan.

For Mehtab and Ram Pyara, the operation was done, and they left soon after.

As soon as the police jeep was out of sight, Saraswati turned towards Karan and screamed, 'What was this? You said everything was fine!'

Karan got up and pulled her into his arms. She tried to break free and started hitting him on the back with her balled-up fists. But Karan was too strong for her. After her anger subsided and she started to cry, he began to kiss her.

Then suddenly, he held her by the shoulders and said, 'This wasn't planned, but this is the best thing that could have happened to us.'

'Have you gone mad? All of us will be arrested now,' retorted Saraswati.

'No, we won't be. I know more about polygraph tests than these policemen.'

She relaxed a little as he told her about the test in detail and how they could fool the machine. In another hour, she finally gave him a half smile and asked, 'But are you 100 per cent sure that your strategy will work?'

Karan turned to look at Rajesh, who was listening to every word, and asked, 'What do you think?'

'Sir, you are never wrong.'

'That's right.' Karan exulted.

Three weeks later, on their scheduled dates, one by one, Saraswati, Karan and Rajesh sat connected to a machine in a forensics laboratory in Delhi and answered the questions, while a computer recorded the changes in their parameters. The examiner was an old man, and he monitored them closely through a glass partition from an adjacent room, as a young technician sat across the interviewees and asked them questions. Seated next to the old man were Sub-Inspector Mehtab and Head Constable Ram Pyara.

Mehtab was confident that their lies would be caught by the machines. That's why when he received a report from the forensics lab that the three of them had cleared the test, he was shocked. He immediately called Ram Pyara and shared the findings with him. His assistant was shocked too.

They could do nothing more now. Therefore, without wanting to, they had to close the case. When Ravi's father learnt that the case had been closed due to want of evidence, he was furious. He filed a petition in court pleading that the case be transferred to the crime branch.

Meanwhile, the results sent a wave of happiness and relief through the hearts and minds of Saraswati, Karan and Rajesh.

Rajesh asked for his seventy thousand and Karan paid him happily. There was nothing left for them to do. The case was closed, and the body was lodged so deep that unless someone dug really deep in exactly that spot, no one would ever find it.

As Rajesh left for his native village in the Arrah district of Bihar for a few weeks, Saraswati started to meet Karan more often and more openly. Her parents also turned a blind eye, and when the people of the village reported sightings of the two lovebirds together, her parents said they had given their approval.

If Sub-Inspector Mehtab Singh Yadav had been taken aback by the failure of the polygraph tests, he was even more shocked when the court issued a writ ordering the case to be transferred to the Crime Branch of the Delhi police. The two were requested to report to the office of Manoj Sharma, DCP (Crime), the very next day.

Manoj Sharma was a bald, dark-complexioned police officer of medium height and with a large paunch. Seen outside his office and not in uniform, he looked like an ordinary ill-exercised businessman. But DCP Sharma had a rare talent. He could read people's minds. Though it was not possible in theory for one human being to read another human being's mind, the DCP's friends and followers considered him an exception.

DCP Sharma patiently heard Sub-Inspector Mehtab Singh and Head Constable Ram Pyara, and after they had finished, he leaned back and took a deep breath.

'Finding the body or locating the missing person is the wrong direction to take. We have to find the motive. The only person who would have been uncomfortable because of the marriage is his wife. I think there's more to her.'

Mehtab nodded.

DCP Sharma continued, 'I have spoken to the SHO of Kapashera, and he has agreed to my proposal of allowing you

CASE #5 : SKELETON IN THE CLOSET

to continue with the case since you know so much. You will be assisted by one head constable from my department.'

'Yes, sir. What about Head Constable Ram Pyara?'

'He is not required.'

Mehtab turned and signalled Ram Pyara to leave, who left after a smart salute.

Then Mehtab asked, 'Where do you want me to start next?'

'Keep an eye on Saraswati. We must involve the cyber cell too and check what Mr Singhal has been up to. I want to know whom he has called since the murder, major bank transactions, his emails and even what he has been browsing on the internet.'

The next morning, Karan was sitting in his office. He was staring at his laptop's screen. His face had contorted and his eyes were wide with terror.

He was staring at the ZIPNet page of the Delhi police. This was an online project of the Delhi police through which common citizens could find out the status of missing persons.

There was nothing specific he could decipher from the page. He was just staring at the picture of Ravi Kumar. The reason for his anxiety was the call he had received moments ago. Someone had tipped him off that Ravi Kumar's case had been transferred to the crime branch.

He had found out more about DCP (Crime) Manoj Sharma, and it was giving him jitters. He reached for his mobile phone and dialled a number.

'Rajesh, come back as soon as you can. It's an emergency; catch a train and come here.'

'Sir, what happened?'

After a pause, he added, 'I can't tell you on the phone. We have to take action quickly, or all three of us will be rotting in jail.'

'Sir, but …'

Karan paused for a few more seconds and then shouted, '*Saale, wapas aa ja kal tak, nahin to* (Return by tomorrow, or else) …'

The next night, as soon as Rajesh arrived at Karan's doorstep, Karan was ready with two shovels. Without a word, both walked to the spot near the warehouse where they had buried Ravi Kumar. Once they were standing there, Karan looked at Rajesh and said, 'The crime branch has got the case now. We need to get rid of the body.'

Rajesh looked at his employer with wide eyes. 'Sir, we already got rid of the body. No one can find it here.'

'You don't know the crime branch. They will bring sniffer dogs and the dogs will bark. Then they will get an earth mower and dig it up.'

Rajesh nodded in understanding and asked, 'So what should we do?'

'We will get the body out and scatter the bones over a large area far away from here. That way, not even the crime branch will be able to put the dead body together. That means no evidence.'

'As you say, sir.'

CASE #5 : SKELETON IN THE CLOSET

With the headlights of Karan's car lighting up the spot, the two started digging. The time was 9 p.m. They had to dig for three hours before one of their shovels hit a bone.

Karan nodded towards the headlights. Rajesh sat behind the wheel and adjusted the car. As soon as the two front wheels crossed the edge of the pit, causing the front to sink lower than the rear and giving them a better view of the pit, Rajesh placed two stones under the rear wheels to hold the vehicle in place. Then, after applying the handbrake, Rajesh got out and joined him. Slowly, they lowered themselves into the pit again and started to tap and dig carefully, working like committed archaeologists who were looking for fossils and taking precautions so that the million-year-old nature-preserved relics were not damaged.

By now, the flesh had decomposed, and they removed as many bones as they could. But before they could finish properly, it was dawn. Scared that the early risers might drift in their direction, they decided to conclude their operation.

After putting all the bones in a gunny bag and placing it in the boot of the car, they covered the pit with soil once again.

Although they were exhausted, they drove towards Rewari in Haryana, and as the sun rose, one by one, they threw the bones over the next fifty-odd kilometres.

After this, they returned in the evening, went to their houses and slept.

Meanwhile, DCP Sharma's request to the cyber-crime office yielded positive results, as did Sub-Inspector Mehtab's request to the SHO of Gelpur to keep Karan and Saraswati under surveillance.

One morning in October 2012, DCP Sharma called Sub-Inspector Mehtab to review the case and decide the further course of action.

As soon as Mehtab was seated, the DCP said, 'First, tell me, what have you got? Because what I have will blow your mind.'

Mehtab started, 'Sir, it has been confirmed that Saraswati is in a physical relationship with Karan.'

'Hmm ... that gives them a motive to remove the obstacle, Ravi Kumar. Well, according to the cyber branch, Karan has been watching movies in which perfect crimes have been committed and the killers have successfully escaped arrest. He has also been doing web searches regarding the police's way of functioning, including the crime branch. Clearly, they had a motive and it was a premeditated murder.'

'Yes, sir. These two should be behind bars.'

The DCP spoke thoughtfully. 'That's right, but the question is how? These findings won't hold water in court. Without knowing where the body is, we can't do much.'

For the next five years, Mehtab tried his best to find more details, but he couldn't get a clue about the missing body. Over time, the DCP also slowed down, and the case became one of those festering wounds that continued to hurt but could not be treated.

Finally, in 2017, Mehtab proposed a new idea to DCP Sharma.

'Sir, since they know they are guilty and have to remain looking over their shoulders all their lives, I can once again play a setting-you-free game with them.'

'Please elaborate.'

Mehtab's eyes brightened as he spoke. 'Sir, let me tell them that if they clear the narco-analysis test, the police will never bother them.'

'What if they clear it like they cleared the polygraph test?'

'That's the thing, sir. I have spoken to the laboratory in Gandhinagar, and they say that it is impossible to escape if they are guilty.'

'Hmm, but will they agree?'

'Sir, leave that to me. I understand this Karan Singhal. I will set him up nicely. This is our only chance.'

'Let me get approval from the court. Once we have it, you can go ahead.'

The crime branch succeeded in convincing the court. A few days later, Mehtab drove to Karan's office in Gelpur once again. It had been five years since his last visit. By now, lots of things had changed. Karan was clearly wealthier, and his cheeks had filled out. Mehtab was informed by the local policeman that Saraswati was living happily with Karan and that she was pregnant.

Saraswati's pregnancy posed a problem for Mehtab, as he knew that now she could not undergo the test. His hopes pinned on Karan, he knocked at his door. Karan recognized him instantly and greeted him with a lot of confidence.

'Sir, welcome. It is a pleasure to see you again.'

'Thank you, Karan ji. I can see that you are doing a lot better now.'

'Yes, sir. All due to your good wishes. And the blessings of God. Please sit.'

'Thank you.'

Just like the previous time, Sub-Inspector Mehtab succeeded in persuading Karan to take the test. He said the police would cover his travel and stay to Gandhinagar and back.

The narco-analysis test, just like the polygraph test, is quite controversial. It's also risky for the well-being of the person being tested. After a court approves the procedure and the person in question consents in writing, the test is conducted by injecting an anaesthetic (usually sodium thiopental) in a quantity sufficient to induce the second stage of anaesthesia, also called the hypnotic state. There are basically four states induced by anaesthesia. The first state is when the person feels drugged but knows what is going on and can think almost clearly; the second state, or the hypnotic state, is a semi-conscious state in which the person starts speaking their thoughts when asked, without understanding the implications; the third state is when the person becomes unconscious and can't communicate at all; and the fourth state is when the person goes into a prolonged coma or dies. These stages are maintained by the anaesthetist by administering the right dosage of drugs and moderating it over time, based on the monitoring of the person's vital signs.

The narco-test is, therefore, conducted with a lot of precautions, and a team of specialists monitors the progress. The finalization of the results also takes a few weeks.

According to the procedure, therefore, when the test was conducted on Karan Singhal, besides the anaesthetist, there was a clinical psychologist, a psychiatrist, nursing staff, a person to log all the details of the orders and the readings of the vitals and a videographer to record everything.

The procedure started, and the anaesthesia was injected into Karan Singhal. He appeared confident. As soon as he reached stage two, Mehtab started to ask him questions, and Karan started to reveal everything about the crime. The Delhi police had scored a bullseye.

A few weeks later, as soon as the results were received by the Delhi police, arrest warrants were issued to arrest Karan, Saraswati and Rajesh. When the police arrived in Gelpur, they found that the three of them were missing.

Rajesh was captured from his village in Bihar three days later. Karan was arrested a week later in Gelpur itself, where he was hiding in a friend's house. Being a businessman, with all his assets and liabilities in that village, the police knew he would emerge from hiding soon, and, therefore, when he did, they pounced on him. Saraswati, who was by now eight months pregnant, could not be found.

The police started by digging up the plot of land that was adjacent to Karan's warehouse. By now, they knew the exact chain of events and were, therefore, aware that the body had been exhumed. Yet, for procedural necessity, they dug deep and were surprised to find a few bones. Clearly, Karan and his driver had not done a thorough job that night. After that, they drove along the highway and conducted a meticulous search. Since more than five years had elapsed, this was a futile exercise. But the persistent efforts of the police resulted in the recovery of numerous bones. When the DNA test was finally conducted, twenty-five of these bones matched the DNA of Ravi Kumar.

The Delhi Police meticulously built an airtight case against Karan Singhal and Rajesh, but capturing Saraswati was crucial to solidifying their case. With all leads exhausted, they announced a reward of 50,000 rupees for any information on Saraswati's whereabouts. In July 2021, a breakthrough came when they received a tip-off about her being spotted in Alwar. Acting swiftly, the police launched a fortnight-long operation, conducting door-to-door searches and setting up roadblocks around the area where she was last seen. Their relentless efforts paid off when Saraswati was finally apprehended and taken into custody.

CASE #6

THE LAST STRAW

Case overview and tools of investigation: By following an ID document's trail and pursuing all leads as evidenced at the crime scene at a hotel in Kolkata, the West Bengal Police succeeded in capturing a serial killer from Jharkhand.

Location: Kolkata, Bankura, Patna, Jamui and Jasidih

On a hot morning in April 2015, twenty-two-year-old Vijay Purohit was seated in a tea shop on the outskirts of Patna and sipping tea, when a young woman walked in with an elderly man.

As soon as the two of them sat down, they began to talk.

His head turned away at an angle from them, Vijay's attention was instantly caught by their conversation.

The woman said, 'Dad, it's good that you have finalized your will at last.'

The father replied, 'Beta, after I'm gone, I don't want you and your sister to fight. God has been kind to me, and I have a lot to leave for both of you.'

The woman pulled a face and said, 'Dad, Babita and I would never fight over your property.'

'I know, I know, but what about Babita's husband? Or your husband when you get married?'

The woman was embarrassed. She rode the wave of shyness for the next few seconds and said, 'Dad, no, please don't talk about my marriage. I will not get married.'

He laughed and said, 'Babita used to say the same thing.'

They paused to sip their teas.

The father was dressed in a neat shirt and trousers. He wore polished leather shoes, and expensive-looking spectacles rested on his nose. The daughter was in tight jeans and a pink top. She was average to look at, and, Vijay thought, had it not been for her figure-hugging clothes, no one would have given her a second look.

At one point, the woman turned and her eyes met Vijay's. He smiled and winked at the woman. She giggled and looked away.

The elderly man's phone began to ring. He stared at the screen, pulled a face and walked away to take the call.

This was Vijay's opportunity. A greedy and ambitious man, Vijay was a jack of all trades but a master of none. He had no steady source of income and no special skill or education. He knew, therefore, that the only way he could become rich was if he partnered with someone who was already rich. Vijay was five feet eight inches tall, stockily built and had a wheatish complexion and a winning smile that never failed to charm people.

Seizing the opportunity, he looked at the woman and said, 'You are not from Patna, I can tell.'

She flicked her head and looked at the stranger who had winked at her earlier. After a momentary pause, she smiled and said, 'No, we are from Jamui.'

Vijay continued to smile.

She asked, 'How did you know?'

Vijay said, 'Because women in Patna aren't so beautiful.'

She laughed. 'You could have given me this compliment straight, instead of beating around the bush. And for your information, I know I'm average, not beautiful.'

'Wrong. People have been lying to you.'

'What about the mirror? Does the mirror lie too?'

'Yes, the mirror tells you what you want to believe.' He winked before continuing, 'But I know you are beautiful. In fact, very beautiful, Miss ...?'

'Sangeeta.'

He closed his eyes and whispered, 'Sangeeta ... what a lovely name.'

'Shut up. I know all about you guys from Patna who know how to charm small-city girls. I want you to stop talking to me now.'

She turned her face away.

He whispered, 'I don't want to talk either. I just want to *look* at you.'

When Sangeeta didn't turn to face him again, Vijay started to hum a song. But a few moments later, as soon as he saw her father return, he stopped.

The father and daughter sat there for a few more minutes without speaking and then left. Vijay followed them and saw them get in a car and drive off. He noted the car's registration number.

The next day, through his contacts at the RTO department in Patna, he found out Sangeeta's address in Jamui. He also learnt her father's name and the fact that he was a reasonably wealthy man.

For the next few nights, Vijay stared at the picture of Sangeeta that he had secretly clicked on his mobile phone at the tea shop. However hard he tried, he knew he wasn't attracted to her. But she had money, and this fact eclipsed all the doubts in his head, making her look reasonably attractive, enough for him to lay out his net.

One of Vijay's peculiar addictions was his obsession with B-grade South Indian films, particularly the ones that showcased outlandish and imaginative methods of committing crimes. These movies fascinated him, often blurring the lines between fiction and reality in his mind. At times, he couldn't help but wonder: Had he merely dreamed of enacting those cinematic crimes during his hazy, blackout nights, or had he actually carried them out? The uncertainty gnawed at him, leaving a chilling question unanswered.

With no job, no prospect and no money, Vijay decided to try his luck with Sangeeta. Within just two weeks of meeting her, he boarded a bus from Patna for Jamui to put his plan into motion. His daily-wage-earning father, mother and brother didn't even ask him where he was going. One person less in the Purohit household meant one less mouth to feed.

The bus covered the 170 kilometres in almost five hours, stopping at places he hadn't heard the names of. Finally, in the afternoon, stiff from sitting in the same position, Vijay got down in Jamui. The scene around him was a disappointment.

Jamui, as he would learn in the coming days, was nothing but an overgrown village.

Vijay knew it would be a risk to go and face Sangeeta straightaway. She would think he was stalking her. He would have to, therefore, play his cards carefully.

Jamui was a small town with a population of around eighty thousand. Vijay walked the length and breadth of the city to get a sense of the place. He figured out quickly that getting a job here would be difficult.

When he found an electrical shop, he told the man behind the counter, 'I'm looking for a job. I can do repairs.'

The owner shook his head and signalled him to leave immediately.

At the next electrical shop, Vijay changed his strategy. 'I want to work in your shop for free for the first month. If you like my work, you can keep me and pay whatever you think I deserve.'

He got the job.

Now he needed a place to live.

The shopkeeper said, 'There is a small room above our shop. You can sleep there.'

'Thank you. You won't be disappointed.'

Vijay knew the basics of electrical repairs, and he was able to impress his new employer over the next two weeks. Once he was comfortable, he took a day off and approached Sangeeta's house.

It was an independent house that was large enough for a joint family of twenty people to live in comfortably. But, by careful observation and by casually speaking to the owner of a paan shop located close by, he found out that it was just Sangeeta, her father, her sister, Babita, Babita's husband, Dharmendra, and their daughter, Jyoti, who lived in the house. Sangeeta's mother had passed away a few years earlier.

In the evening, he saw Sangeeta leaving the house. She walked a short distance before hailing a cycle rickshaw. Vijay started to follow her in another rickshaw. Ten minutes later, Sangeeta got down at the market. Vijay did the same, and as she walked the narrow lanes of the market, Vijay guessed her movements and overtook her from a side lane. Then he surprised her by appearing suddenly from the opposite side. He flashed her his winning smile.

Sangeeta took a second to recognize him. 'You?'

Vijay feigned surprise. 'Oh, hello! We met in Patna, didn't we?'

She folded her arms across her chest and said, 'And you followed me here?'

'Of course not. I got a job a few days earlier. Didn't I say I was an electrician?'

She shook her head. 'No, you didn't.'

It was his turn to fold his arms, and he said, trying to imitate her, 'Well, I declare it now. I'm the greatest electrician in Jamui.'

She laughed, and after exchanging a few more sentences, she gave him her number.

Over the next few weeks, Vijay and Sangeeta started to meet regularly. As they got closer with each meeting, it wasn't difficult for Vijay to convince Sangeeta that they were meant for each other.

Within the next six months, Vijay and Sangeeta were married. His parents came from Patna to attend the wedding and left feeling relieved that they no longer had to worry about their unemployed son. His brother couldn't attend due to his work.

After getting married, the first thing Vijay did was quit his job and shift into Sangeeta's house.

Before Vijay could set his plan of making money off Sangeeta into motion, one evening Sangeeta's father had a massive heart attack. He was rushed to the hospital, but he passed away. While the family was mourning, Vijay realized it was now only a matter of time before half the property would be transferred to Sangeeta's name. He knew about the existence of the will because he had heard about it when Sangeeta and her father had discussed it in Patna.

A few days later, Vijay brought this up with Sangeeta. 'Darling, now that your father is no more, you sisters must get his properties transferred to your names.'

She nodded and said, 'Yes, you are right. But I don't have much to do with this, because Dad has given most of his property to Babita didi.'

Vijay was shocked, and he said, 'Most to her? But why? Aren't you his daughter too?'

She smiled and replied, 'Of course I am, but here in Jamui, in our community, there is a custom of giving most of the property to the eldest child.'

Vijay frowned and said, 'But that's not fair. How will we live our lives now?'

She raised her eyebrows and spoke, slightly irritated for the first time. 'What do you mean by this? You are my husband and you will earn.'

'Oh!' He got up and walked away as a shadow of worry crossed Sangeeta's face.

That night, Vijay couldn't sleep. He realized that not only did he not have the money, but his non-beautiful wife was a liability as well. His thoughts turned to Dharmendra, his brother-in-law, who would get all the money and had the better-looking sister as his wife. Seething with jealousy and anger, Vijay decided that he must replace Dharmendra with himself. Babita was rich, so he believed he deserved her more than Dharmendra.

Dharmendra was a businessman whose business, at that time, was not doing well. He was dark-complexioned and had a big paunch, and his general appearance was unpleasant. Babita wasn't a beauty either, but she was more well-endowed than her sister and had a very sweet voice.

By morning, Vijay knew what to do. Neither Babita nor Sangeeta knew the real Vijay. In fact, no one in the world knew about the experiments he had conducted on a few people in Patna and nearby villages. Now the time had come to do something drastic to save his future. He wondered once again if those dreams were true. Part of his mind whispered that they indeed were.

As a first step, he started to get close to Babita. It was surprisingly easy, as she seemed to like his attention and encouraged him. The teasing soon gave way to kissing, and finally, one afternoon, while Dharmendra was out of town on business, Sangeeta was at the market and Jyoti was asleep after school, Vijay and Babita made love. Just as Vijay was about to climax, their sounds woke Jyoti up, and she saw them naked.

As Vijay got dressed, Babita told Jyoti, 'You are too young to understand what you saw. I don't want you to talk about this to anyone, okay?'

The wide-eyed girl nodded.

Vijay left the room and lay down on his bed. His problems were multiplying. Extra people were standing in the way of his money. All he needed was Babita; the other three were unnecessary baggage.

Two days later, when Dharmendra returned from his trip, he looked sad. Vijay took him out that evening and bought expensive whisky for both of them.

Vijay poured his co-brother a drink and asked, 'What's wrong, Dharmendra ji? You look worried.'

Dharmendra took a sip and said, 'It's nothing.'

Vijay gave him his winning smile and said, 'You know what, if you tell me your problem, I will fix it. My friends used to call me Mr Fixer. I know so many people—'

'You think I'm an asshole?'

'No. Why would you say that?'

'Don't give me gyan. If you are such a fixer, why don't you fix your own problems? You don't even have a job. At least I'm trying to do something.'

Vijay was so angry that he wanted to smash the bottle on Dharmendra's head right then and there. But he controlled himself and said, 'You are right.'

'I'm sorry. I shouldn't have said that ... Actually, I'm in a crisis.'

Vijay poured him another drink and said, 'Don't tell me about your problem if you don't want to.'

Dharmendra inhaled deeply. 'I'm in a lot of debt, brother. It's not because my business acumen is poor. It's because a party in Bankura has not cleared their dues for the last two years.'

'Oh! Can I say something that might be useful to you?'

'Okay.'

'No, only if you want me to.'

'Look, I'm sorry, Vijay. Tell me—what can Mr Fixer do?'

Vijay poured him another drink and said, 'Well, I can get your money in one day. Guaranteed.'

'But how?'

'That's why they call me Mr Fixer.'

Dharmendra looked uncertain as he seemed to be making up his mind. Finally, he said, 'What do you need from my side?'

'Just the name of the party. And after that, we will both go there and collect the money.'

'That's it?'

'That's it!'

He started to laugh. Vijay looked at him, smiling outwardly but very angry on the inside.

Finally, Vijay said, 'Look, brother, all I want you to do is trust me. I'll go to Bankura with you, we will stay for one day and we will come back with the money.'

'Okay.'

The next morning, Dharmendra gave Vijay the name of the party that was defaulting on the payment. Vijay did nothing about the name. Instead, he convinced his wife, Sangeeta, to go with them to Bankura, promising to show her around. Sangeeta agreed. She insisted they take Jyoti along too, as her school holidays were going on, to which Vijay agreed. When Babita expressed her interest to join them, Vijay convinced her that it was not safe for all of them to lock the house and just leave. She agreed to stay back.

On 1 October 2015, they took a bus from Jamui to Bankura in West Bengal. The distance was around 290 kilometres, and it took them eight hours to reach Bankura town. As they travelled, Jyoti was the happiest. Wherever the bus stopped, Sangeeta pampered her niece and bought her drinks and snacks that she demanded.

Vijay and Dharmendra didn't speak much. While Dharmendra slept during most of the journey, Vijay's mind was busy planning his next move. All he could see in his mind's eye was Babita as his wife and none of the present occupants of the bus anywhere in sight.

After getting down in Bankura, Vijay pulled Dharmendra to one side and said, 'Let's first book a room for Sangeeta and Jyoti in a hotel. After that, you and I will go to another hotel, where your party will bring the money.'

'This is your plan, Vijay. Let's do whatever works best.'

They went to a hotel that was close to the bus stop, and while Dharmendra waited in the reception area, Vijay used his voter ID card to check Sangeeta and Jyoti in. After that, Vijay and Dharmendra left the hotel.

Ten minutes later, they checked into another hotel. Here too, Vijay used his voter ID card to check in.

After they settled in their room, Dharmendra said, 'We could have taken another room in the same hotel that Sangeeta and Jyoti are in.'

Vijay said, 'I don't think that is a good idea. Look, I have found out about your party, and they are not very good people. I, therefore, don't expect them to behave straight.'

'Oh!'

'But don't worry—my guy who will escort them here will take care of everything.'

'Meaning?'

'Meaning if they have guns on them, he will get them deposited and then bring them to the room.'

Dharmendra nodded. He was beginning to look uncertain, and Vijay knew this was not a good sign.

It was 8 p.m. now. Vijay called a number and faked a conversation. 'We are ready ... No, no half payment—we want full payment.'

He pretended to listen for a few seconds, his face hardening, and then said, 'No hanky-panky; let's exchange the money and go our ways. No one needs to get hurt.'

From the corner of his eye, he saw Dharmendra stiffen.

'See you at ten.'

Vijay pretended to disconnect and looked at him. He smiled and pulled out the bottle of whisky he was carrying in his bag. Then he picked up two glasses and poured generous pegs.

Dharmendra picked up a glass and finished it in one go. Vijay poured him another one. And then another. By now, Dharmendra was getting his confidence back, so much so that he started to brag. 'Vijay, I'm happy that you are helping me with this case. I know a lot of people too … If you ever get into trouble in Jamui, just let me know.'

'I surely will.'

Dharmendra got to his feet and went to the bathroom. This was Vijay's moment. He made another peg for Dharmendra and added some powder from a small plastic pouch that he was carrying in his pocket. He stirred it quickly.

Dharmendra came out, took a sip and said, his voice slurring, 'How much more time for them to come?'

Vijay smiled and said, 'I got a message while you were in the bathroom. Fifteen more minutes.'

He nodded and kept sipping his whisky. Vijay was observing him closely now.

After a few more sips, the glass slipped out of Dharmendra's hand and he closed his eyes. Vijay waited for the drugs to spread through his enemy's body and deactivate his senses.

Half an hour later, he picked up his gamchha and wrapped it around Dharmendra's neck. Then he started to strangle the unconscious enemy. The body struggled, but Vijay kept his hold firm. A few minutes later, it was all over.

After this, Vijay left the room and walked out of the hotel.

Vijay then arrived at the room where his wife, Sangeeta, and his niece, Jyoti, were staying.

Sangeeta embraced him as soon as he came into the room and said, 'I'm so tired and hungry. What took you so long?'

'Sorry, darling, I was meeting someone.'

'And where is Dharmendra?'

'He had to suddenly leave for Kolkata. From there, he will take a flight to Delhi. He said there's been some sudden development in his work.'

'Oh!'

Let's just eat now and go to sleep. Tomorrow morning, we will also leave for Kolkata.'

They ate dinner and slept.

The next morning, they took a bus from Bankura to Kolkata. The distance was 220 kilometres, and it took them six hours to reach Kolkata. In Kolkata, they checked into a hotel. This time too, Vijay used his voter ID card for the check-in.

'Uncle, when will we go sightseeing?' It was Jyoti who asked as soon as they had settled in the room. It was late evening by now.

'Tomorrow morning, I promise.' Vijay smiled at her.

'Okay, uncle.' She smiled back.

They unpacked and rested a while. After that, Vijay ordered dinner for all three of them.

Sangeeta exclaimed, 'I feel so tired, Vijay!'

Vijay took out the drug pouch from his pocket and added its contents to a glass of water, extending it towards Sangeeta. 'Take this for instant energy.'

Sangeeta drank it in one go. By the time the food arrived at around 8 p.m., Sangeeta was feeling drowsy.

Vijay looked at her and said, 'You are so sleepy, honey. Eat this dinner and then rest.'

Somehow, Sangeeta ate a little, but she was not able to keep her eyes open. Vijay helped her into bed. After this, Vijay and Jyoti ate silently. Finally, Vijay put Jyoti to bed too and sat down in a chair to wait.

At midnight, he opened his bag and took out a bundle of copper wires. Then he removed all the clothes Sangeeta was wearing and wrapped her body in copper wires. He was excited to carry out this experiment that he had seen in a South Indian movie, and his eyes gleamed with child-like enthusiasm.

Vijay placed her naked body wrapped in copper wires on the floor to turn it into a conductor. The wires were connected to the socket and ready. Now all he had to do was switch the power supply on. He inhaled deeply, allowed the image of Babita to float into his mind, smiled and flicked the switch. The body started to squirm, but the eyes remained closed. He just sat there and watched.

Just then, he noticed Jyoti had woken up. She looked at her aunt's naked body wrapped in wires on the floor and said, 'Uncle, what are you doing?'

This was not a good sign. Vijay slapped the girl so hard that she was knocked unconscious before she fell to the floor. He then wrapped her body in copper wires too and did the same with her. There was no way he would let her live after what she had seen. What if she told the police? That would ruin his beautiful future with Babita.

After they were dead, Vijay walked out of the room. He had used a voter ID card to check in, but he knew there was nothing to worry about, as he had snatched this card from a man in Patna a year ago.

From Kolkata, Vijay took a bus to Jasidih, a small town of around fifteen thousand people in Jharkhand that was located 320 kilometres from Kolkata. Vijay knew the murders would create a lot of heat, and he needed to be away from the scene of the crime and the location the victims belonged to—Bankura, Kolkata and Jamui.

The first thing he did after the bus started to move was switch off his mobile.

The black phone on Inspector Binoy Pradhan's desk rang at midday the next day. The police station was located a few hundred metres from the hotel.

He picked it up and said, 'Inspector Pradhan speaking.'

After listening for a few seconds, he said, 'Calm down; tell me the name of the hotel. Okay, we are on our way.'

Inspector Binoy Pradhan and two constables were at the hotel in less than ten minutes. They were received by the manager.

The manager said, 'Sir, this way.'

When they approached the scene of the crime on the second floor, they encountered a strange smell. When they stepped inside the room, they found the bodies of two victims, a woman in her early twenties and a girl aged around ten. The victims had burn marks on their bodies due to the copper wires.

Inspector Binoy Pradhan had never seen anything like this in his life. He had seen many murders, including some very gruesome ones, but this was altogether on a different level. He got the area cordoned off and put in a request for the assistance of the Forensics Science Laboratory. Based on his brief report, his request was approved, and the bodies were taken away for postmortem after the crime scene had been properly photographed.

CASE #6: THE LAST STRAW

At the Kolkata police headquarters in Lalbazar, taking cognizance of the gruesome nature of the double murders, the case was transferred to the detective department.

By 3 p.m., the Joint Commissioner of Police (Crime), Shambhunath Gaurav, was at the scene of crime. Six feet tall, Shambhunath was an IPS officer of the 1997 batch. A sharp observer, he was a short-tempered man in his early fifties who believed in the use of technology to solve crimes and was tech-savvy, unlike many officers of his age.

A few journalists had arrived at the hotel by then, and they were moving about everywhere. It looked like someone from the hotel had informed the media.

After a quick inspection of the scene of crime, the JCP (Crime) pulled Inspector Binoy Pradhan to one side and asked, 'Why is the media here?'

'Sir, the manager doesn't know it yet, but someone from the hotel, who doesn't understand the implications, did this.'

'Okay, so what's your initial impression of the case?'

Inspector Binoy said, 'Sir, three people checked in last evening. Two of them are dead and the third one is missing. We have taken a copy of the voter ID card that he used to check in.'

'His name and address?'

'Sir, his name is Ram Ashray Verma and he is from Patna.'

Inspector Binoy showed him the copy of the voter ID card. The JCP glanced at it and returned it to him.

'Sir, it's an open-and-shut case.'

'Did you find any IDs on the victims?'

'No, sir.'

'So, we don't know their names?'

'We don't.'

'You think the victims and the killer are related?'

'Most likely, sir. Otherwise, people would have noticed something amiss when they checked in. Once we have this Verma character in our custody, we will find out more.'

'This case needs interstate cooperation with Bihar, which I will get organized. Now onwards, the homicide section of the Detective department will investigate this case, okay?'

'Yes, sir.'

'I'll send someone soon to take over the crime scene and all evidence from you.'

'Yes, sir.'

By 8 p.m., standing before Inspector Binoy Pradhan was Inspector Jogen Sanyal of the homicide department. He was accompanied by two Sub-Inspectors named Mukul Haldar and Asit Ghosal. Within the next two hours, as ordered, the local police station handed over the case to the homicide section of the detective department.

Jogen was a short man of around five feet five inches. He was slim and wore round spectacles that gave an impression that he was perhaps a teacher or a painter or even an artist. Contrary to the first impression he created, when he opened his mouth, everything changed. He had a baritone that was as smooth as it was deep and commanding. He was intelligent, experienced and a decorated officer of the Kolkata police. Mukul and Asit had been working under him for the last five years and desperately wanted to work under someone else because Jogen was not only a hard taskmaster but also unpredictable.

Six feet tall and aged around forty, Mukul was an average man who loved football and classic movies more than his job. He was also a secret blogger who extensively chronicled these subjects online.

Asit was five feet nine inches tall, aged thirty and a keen learner, but Mukul had convinced him that they were already working above their paygrades because of Jogen. But neither could voice their opinions or disagreements in front of their boss. Therefore, whenever Jogen was not around, Mukul complained nonstop and Asit kept nodding.

After inspecting the scene of the crime and the evidence bags had been handed over to Jogen, Inspector Binoy Pradhan left with his team. Jogen watched them go, his face as opaque as ever. Both Mukul and Asit knew Jogen would now embrace this investigation as if his life depended on it. They knew what this meant—their coming days and weeks, maybe even months, would be taken up by this investigation.

Both saw Jogen walk to one corner of the room and close his eyes. They kept theirs open, waiting, sulking and in suspense about what would come next.

Jogen opened his eyes and looked in their direction. He said, 'So, what should be our first course of action?'

Mukul replied, 'Sir, we should ask the Bihar police to arrest the killer from Patna. And the forensic lab should compare his fingerprints when he is brought here with the fingerprints we have collected from the scene of the crime—this room.'

Jogen looked at Asit.

Asit said, 'Yes, sir. Mukul sir is right.'

Jogen walked up to him. He said, 'When will you two grow up? You think the killer will be sitting at his Patna address and waiting for the police to show up because his ID is here at the hotel?'

Both looked at him and blinked.

'These murders have taken place in Kolkata, not in Bihar. We will go there and look for the killer. The Bihar police will help, but we will lead this investigation. How can someone kill a woman and a young girl right here in a prime area of Kolkata and disappear?'

'Yes, sir,' Mukul and Asit chimed in chorus.

The same evening, the three of them took a flight to Patna. They were received by a head constable of the Bihar police at the airport, who drove them straight to Ram Ashray Verma's address as printed on the voter ID card.

In the jeep, Jogen asked Mukul, 'Do you think we will find our killer there?'

'No, sir.'

'Then why are we going there?'

'It's a good starting point, sir.'

Jogen stared at him and said, 'Right.'

Mukul looked at Asit and gave him a half smile. Asit nodded and smiled back.

Ram Ashray Verma was a man of around fifty. He was wearing pyjama bottoms and a vest when he opened the door of his house, simultaneously scratching his crotch and yawning. When he saw three strangers standing in front of his door and a policeman in uniform, he smiled uncertainly and said, 'Sir?'

Jogen said, 'Are you Ram Ashray Verma?'

'Yes, sir.'

'When did you return from Kolkata?'

'Kolkata? I have never been to Kolkata in my life, sir …'

Jogen looked at Asit, who pulled out a copy of the voter ID. Jogen took it from him and extended it towards Ram Ashray.

Ram Ashray looked at the copy and said, 'Sir, someone had snatched my voter ID a year ago.'

'Did you report it to the police?'

'No, sir.'

'Hmm … where were you during the last three days?'

'I was right here with my wife, my mother and my fifteen-year-old son. I have a daughter also, who is eight.'

Jogen and the others met the family members and realized that Ram Ashray was speaking the truth.

'So who was this man who stole your card?'

'Sir, he collided with me in the market. My wallet fell on the road and flew open. Before I could pick it up, he grabbed the voter card that had slipped out.'

'And?'

'And I asked him to please return it to me, but the man said he needed it more than me. Then he ran away.'

'Can you describe him?'

'Sir, what has that man done? Where did you get this copy?'

Jogen looked at the head constable from the Bihar police, who nodded, got up and slapped Ram Ashray hard. Ram Ashray fell from his chair.

The head constable said, 'Answer what is being asked. These people have come from West Bengal. Don't spoil the image of Bihar. Understood?'

Ram Ashray nodded, got up from the floor and sat back in the chair again.

Jogen repeated the question: 'Can you describe the man?'

This time, Ram Ashray started giving the impression of the man who had stolen his ID. By now, Asit was already video recording what was being said on his mobile.

After ten minutes, they were back in the jeep again.

Jogen asked Mukul, 'Do you think he's speaking the truth?'

Mukul hesitated, wondering what he should say so that his boss would not mock him. 'Sir, I think … well, I think … he might be—not sure, though, but …'

'Shut up!' said Jogen and turned towards Asit. 'That man is speaking the truth. Send the video to our department and tell them I need the sketch in two hours.'

Mukul spoke, sounding as underconfident as ever. 'Sir, I was about to say the same thing.'

Jogen didn't respond or even look at him. His eyes were straight on the road.

Jogen, Mukul and Asit returned to Kolkata the next morning. By the time they reached the scene of the crime at around one in the afternoon, the sketch printouts of the suspect had been distributed to the hotel's staff and to the informers and snack vendors at Howrah railway station and nearby bus stops.

At three, they had their second lead. A jhalmuri snack seller had spotted a non-Bengali-speaking trio of a man in his twenties, a woman in her twenties and a girl around ten disembark from a bus that came from Bankura three days ago.

Mukul received this information on his phone, and he relayed it to Jogen.

CASE #6: THE LAST STRAW

Jogen stared at him and asked, 'What do you think we should do?'

Mukul, who had been expecting appreciation for getting this information, looked on, confused, before saying, 'Sir, we should speak to this man.'

'So do it.'

Mukul left for the bus stand along with Asit, while Jogen stayed back in the hotel's lobby. He now had more questions for the manager.

Mukul was excited that he was leading the investigation now with Asit by his side. On arrival at the bus stand, they spoke to the vendor.

Mukul said, 'I'm Sub-Inspector Mukul Haldar from the detective department, homicide section. This here is my assistant, Sub-Inspector Asit Ghosal.'

The vendor was a frail young man of around thirty who had short hair resembling a porcupine that had been alarmed. He smiled and frowned at the same time, in awe due to the fact that two policemen had driven to meet him and were now asking for his help.

He managed to say, 'Sir, would you like to eat some jhalmuri first?'

Mukul smiled, wondering how Jogen would have reacted in a situation like this. He would have certainly hated it and shouted at the vendor. But Mukul was different.

Mukul smiled and said, 'Yes, two portions for both of us.'

Asit looked at him and asked, 'Sir, really?'

Mukul ignored Asit.

The vendor prepared two portions while the policemen waited. After they had accepted the snack in newspaper cones, the vendor started, 'Sir, I'm not sure it was the same person in the sketch, but he was with a woman and a girl. They were not Bengalis. I know because I tried to sell them jhalmuri and they spoke to me in Hindi. Then the man asked me where they could find a decent hotel for the night.'

Mukul spoke while munching. 'So you sent them to that hotel?'

'No, sir. I just told him the area.'

'And they got down from the bus that came from Bankura, right?'

'Yes, sir.'

'What time?'

'Sir, around 6 p.m.'

Mukul opened his wallet and gave him some money. The vendor hesitated, but Mukul insisted with his eyes and the vendor accepted.

From the bus stop, Mukul called Jogen, 'Sir, I think the killer brought the victims from Bankura.'

'So what should we do next?'

This time Mukul knew how to answer. He confidently said, 'Sir, Asit and I will go to Bankura for further investigations.'

'Wrong. What will I do here? Who is the leader of this investigation?'

'Sir, you are.'

'When will you learn to be a good detective, Mukul?'

The call was disconnected. Asit looked at Mukul and asked, 'Sir, is everything okay?'

He nodded, and both walked out of the bus stop.

Meanwhile, Jogen had also got sketches of the victims made based on the photographs they had clicked at the scene of the crime. The victims were still in the mortuary of the government hospital, as no one had come forward to claim the bodies in response to the publication of the pictures in the local newspaper.

When Jogen, Mukul and Asit arrived in Bankura, they had no idea where to start their search from. So, equipped with the sketches of the killer and the victims, they started with the bus stop itself.

What the Kolkata police was clueless about was the fact that the police in Bankura had been grappling with a murder in one of the hotels in the city for the last four days. The man killed was called Dharmendra, and he was from a small town called Jamui in Bihar.

When the evening's work didn't yield positive results, Jogen and his team decided to retire to the police guest house. The next morning, Jogen visited the SP's office for a formal reporting.

The SP listened to him patiently and said, 'We also have an unsolved murder that took place in one of our hotels. This victim was from Bihar too. In fact, our team has just returned from Jamui.'

'Sir, are you suggesting these two could be connected?'

'Probably not. Because the victims were killed in different cities, and the method of killing was different too. But still, do have a word with our Sub-Inspector. His name is Bijoy Haldar.'

'Sure, sir.'

'And do let me know if you need anything. We are here to help Kolkata police in whichever way we can.'

'Thank you, sir.'

As Jogen stepped out of the SP's office, he saw an inspector waiting to go inside. The name plate on the inspector's uniform read 'Bijoy Haldar'.

Jogen nodded at Bijoy, but before he could speak to him, the inspector opened the door and entered the SP's office.

Jogen sat down on the sofa outside and decided to wait.

Bijoy came out after fifteen minutes. He looked at Jogen and asked, 'Are you Inspector Jogen Sanyal?'

Jogen, who was in plain clothes, replied, 'Yes.'

Bijoy sat on another sofa and said, 'SP sir told me you are here.'

Jogen laid out the victims' and the killer's pictures on the table between them. Bijoy picked them up, looked at them closely and then picked up his mobile phone. He compared the sketches with something on his phone. After a few seconds, he looked up and said, 'These two cases are connected.'

'How?'

Bijoy extended his phone towards Jogen.

Jogen looked at the pictures on it—pictures of the victims, taken when they were alive.

In the next few minutes, they discussed the facts they had collectively found and had the bigger picture. Four people of a family had set out from Jamui for Bankura. One of them was killed in Bankura; the other three travelled to Kolkata, where two more were killed. The killer was the same who struck in both cities and was now missing.

Jogen now had a picture of him and a name. He also had a telephone number.

'We have tried this number many times, but it is switched off,' said Bijoy.

Jogen tried it too and discovered that it was off.

After leaving the SP's office, Jogen called Mukul. 'Where are you guys?'

'Sir, we are going with the sketches to hotels and shops near the bus stand.'

'No need. You meet me at the guest house. I'll brief you there.'

Jogen arrived at the guest house and found his assistants waiting. They seemed anxious, and he decided to bring them up to speed right away.

After he had told them all the details, Mukul asked, 'Sir, what's next?'

'That's my question. Who is the boss?'

'Sir, you are.'

'So tell me—what should we do next?'

'Sir, we should return to Kolkata tomorrow morning and start monitoring the telephone number of this Vijay Purohit.'

'Why not leave right now?'

'Sir?'

'Fifteen minutes. That's all both of you have to pack and meet me in the car below.'

With that, Jogen entered his room. After a second's delay, Mukul and Asit dashed to their rooms too.

Meanwhile, Vijay was in Jasidih, biding time. His phone was off, and he had been using another phone with a new SIM. On the TV, he had been following the news about the Kolkata double murders meticulously. Surprisingly, there wasn't much the police was doing. Just like the crimes he had carried out in Patna and nearby villages, he was sure he would get away with these crimes too.

He had been resisting calling Babita. But now, since it had been more than ten days, he decided to call her.

'Babita, my queen, how are you?'

There was alarm in Babita's voice when she replied. 'Vijay, where are you? The police were here. They said Dharmendra is dead. I don't know what's happening. Where are Jyoti and Sangeeta? Why is your phone off?'

'Hey, calm down. All is well. I lost my phone. Sangeeta and Jyoti are fine.'

'I want to talk to Jyoti. Call her to the phone.'

'Wait, listen. I will tell you the truth. After Dharmendra left for Delhi, I travelled to Kolkata with Sangeeta and Jyoti, but one day in the market, I lost them.'

Babita started to cry and spoke through sobs. 'What? What are you saying? Did you go to the police?'

'No, the police are useless. I thought Sangeeta and Jyoti would find their way to Jamui if they didn't find me.'

Babita started to cry more bitterly. She spoke, her voice weak and breaking. 'You killed them, Vijay. I know you killed them.'

Vijay disconnected the phone. Then he threw it against the wall and it broke into pieces.

He turned the TV on but found that he needed to recharge the cable subscription. He picked up his old phone and switched it on to charge the subscription. It took him just a few minutes. After that, he went and threw the phone into a nearby canal and once again turned his attention to the news in Kolkata.

Asit's phone rang in Kolkata's detective department. He looked at the unknown number on the screen, paused for a few seconds and took the call.

'Yes?'

'Sub-Inspector Asit Ghosal?'

'Who is this?'

'Sir, we are calling from Airtel. The number you had given us was briefly activated a few minutes ago.'

Asit's eyes widened. 'Yes, what's the location?'

In the next few minutes, Asit was standing in front of Jogen, Mukul by his side.

'Sir, we have got him.'

Jogen smiled and said, 'I knew I could trust you, Asit.'

'Thank you, sir.'

He looked at Mukul and said, 'Learn something from your junior.'

The next day, Vijay was arrested in Jasidih by Mukul and Asit and brought to Kolkata. On the way, Mukul asked him, 'Why did you do this?'

Vijay smiled and said, 'Do what?'

'Murder your own wife, your niece and your brother-in-law?'

Vijay smiled and said, 'There are twenty-four other people I have killed.'

Mukul and Asit glanced at each other and then Mukul asked, 'When and where?'

'Why should I tell you? I watched South Indian movies and learnt how to kill them. Why don't you watch the same movies and become better cops?'

Mukul wasn't sure how to react to this.

Asit bent forward in the jeep and slapped him. After that, he hissed, 'Shut up!'

Jogen and his team prepared an irrefutable case against Vijay Purohit using the technological evidence they had. The case is currently being heard in court.

CASE #7

THE BUCK STOPS HERE

Case overview and tools of investigation: CCTV footage sharing of intelligence with other states led to the capture of an interstate cybercrime bluff master who had as many as seven aliases.

Location: Hyderabad, Delhi, Jhansi, Patiala and Bikaner.

At ten on a Monday morning, thirty-year-old Divya Jyothi was asleep. Her mother, Vasundhara, knocked on her bedroom door, waited for a few seconds and, on not getting a response, pushed the door open.

Inside the bedroom, Divya was sleeping peacefully. Vasundhara looked at her and pulled a face before saying, 'My sleeping beauty, it's eleven in the morning. Get up now!'

Divya opened one eye, ignored her mother and picked up her mobile phone. She discovered that the time was ten. She closed her eyes again and whispered, 'Mom, it's just ten. Let me sleep for some more time. Please.'

Vasundhara sat on the edge of the bed and caressed her daughter's hair. Lines of worry formed on her face. After a few minutes, tears started to flow from her eyes. She sat there, watching her daughter sleep.

Finally, as she got up to go, Divya caught hold of Vasundhara's hand. She noticed that her mother had been crying silently.

'Mom, please don't worry. Everything is going to be okay.'

'I'm sorry, honey. I know it is going to be okay. But …' She paused to wipe her tears. 'You turned thirty last week and …' She started to cry loudly now.

Divya sat up and hugged her mother. Then she spoke over her shoulder. 'Mom, don't worry, I will get a job soon and then I will get married.'

Vasundhara held her daughter by the shoulders and eased her back to arm's length so that they were face to face. She looked into her eyes, and said, 'Promise me you will get married this year.'

'Yes, Mom. I will.'

She shook her shoulders. 'No. Promise me.'

'Okay, Mom, I promise. Are you happy now?'

Tears flowing from her eyes, Vasundhara tried to smile.

Later, at the breakfast table, as Vasundhara served hot pesarattu dosa, Divya ate while reading the newspaper.

Divya and Vasundhara lived on the fourth floor of a high-rise in Hyderabad. Divya's father had passed away, and she had no siblings. The only source of income for Divya and her mother was what Divya had been earning. But two months ago, she had been laid off by the IT company she worked for.

After she had been laid off, Divya had reached out to her friends and ex-colleagues with a request to refer her for a suitable job, but no opportunities had come her way. Despite her protests, her mother had asked for help from their relatives too, but her efforts had failed to elicit a positive response.

Right now, therefore, she was jobless and in desperate need of work so that they wouldn't have to dig deeper into the savings they had put aside for a rainy day.

The year was 2018, and the month was December. The weather had become pleasant, and people were out in the open, paying visits to their relatives, enjoying day picnics and eating out at restaurants.

While sipping tea, a small advertisement in the newspaper caught her attention.

Urgently looking for suitable candidates for mid-management positions in an IT company in verticals like HR, operations, programming, administration, etc. Candidates with BTech in IT or MCA can apply. Salary will match industry standards and six years' experience is desirable, but not mandatory for suitable candidate.

The advertisement was followed by an email id. Divya placed her cup on the table and straightened her back.

She re-read the advertisement. This was a good opportunity, and her eight years of HR experience with a single company would go to her credit. She also had strong referrals.

Divya brought her laptop from the bedroom, and within the next ten minutes, she had applied for the job. She got an instant reply that her application had been received and if she was shortlisted, someone would get in touch with her soon.

After this, Divya walked to the balcony and stood there, watching children play in the park below. When the sun started to hurt, she stepped inside and made a cup of coffee for her mother and herself.

As soon as she handed the cup of coffee to her mother, she received a notification on her phone. It was a WhatsApp message from an unknown number.

She took a sip and opened the message. By the time she finished reading it, she was smiling ear to ear.

'What is it, Divya?'

'Mom, my application has been shortlisted for a job I applied for.'

'Wow! So you have got this job?'

'No, Mom, had I got the job, I would have jumped on you by now. What this means is I'm one step closer to getting it. I'm one of the few people who will be interviewed for this job.'

'Interview? That's good, but when is the interview?'

'They haven't given a date. But it should be soon because the advertisement said they need people urgently.'

Vasundhara closed her eyes and folded her hands towards the picture of God that hung from the wall in her room. 'Dear God, please give success to my Divya.'

At seven that evening, Divya's phone rang. The caller ID flashed a name: Jay Sharma.

She picked it up. 'Hello?'

A pleasant male voice came on the line. 'Hello, am I talking to Miss Divya Jyothi?'

'Yes, this is Divya Jyothi.'

'Oh, hello. My name is Jay Sharma. I'm calling from New Delhi. It's regarding your job application.'

'Yes, sir. I applied for the job.'

'Yes, great. We like what's on your resume, and our screening committee has cleared you for the interview. Are you available for the interview immediately?'

'Yes, sir. I'm ready for the interview.'

'Wonderful. I'll text you the address for the interview in Delhi.'

'Delhi?'

'Yes, the interview is in Delhi. Is that a problem?'

'No, sir, I mean ...'

'Oh yes, of course, you would like to know more about the company. That's very much in order and, in fact, I should have informed you right in the beginning. Our company is called Jumbo Informatics Private Limited. We are a mid-sized IT company located in Noida, with around two hundred people working for our international clients, mainly in the States and Canada. We are planning to open a branch in Hyderabad soon, followed by Bangalore and Pune in the coming months. We want to consider you for the Hyderabad branch. Any questions?'

'No, sir. But I'm sorry, coming to Delhi could be a bit of an issue.'

'That's all right. We have shortlisted five candidates for the HR position. If you change your mind, do let me know so that I can send you your flight tickets and one day's five-star hotel accommodation in Delhi. Best wishes, Miss Divya. Bye.'

'Sir, wait—'

Divya stared at the phone.

Her mother was looking at her.

'What happened?'

'Mom, they want me to go to Delhi for the interview.'

'Oh, and the job is in Delhi too?'

'No, the job is in Hyderabad. They are opening a new office here.'

'That's good, no?'

Divya thought for a while and said, 'Mom, it's good, but I haven't heard the name of this company before. Let me first check it out.'

'Right.'

Divya looked up the name of the company on her laptop and found its website. The website seemed impressive and had lots of information. There was no doubt—the company was legitimate, and that's why they had even offered to pay for her flight tickets and stay.

She looked up.

Her mother said, 'What?'

'The company is good. It's new but growing fast. I think it's an ideal place for me to start working.'

'Then go for the interview. Don't worry about the travel and the hotel cost. I have got some money saved.'

'Mom, that's not the problem. The guy who called said the company will pay for the flight and the hotel stay upfront.'

Her mother beamed. 'So what's the problem? We don't have to spend for the interview, and the job location is in Hyderabad.'

Divya said, 'I'm not sure, Mom. These days there are so many fraudsters and job scammers in the market.'

'But you said this is a legit company.'

'Yes, it is, but—'

'It's good to be cautious, but you are being overcautious, Divya. You must go. Okay, if it helps you feel more comfortable, I can come with you to Delhi. We don't have to spend for the hotel, just my travel, and, as I said, I have the money for it.'

Divya smiled. 'Yes, Mom. That's a good idea. Let's go together.'

She then called the number she had received the call from. But her call wasn't answered.

Divya spent the whole evening staring at the silent phone. Finally, at around midnight, upset with herself for not saying yes immediately, she fell into a disturbed sleep.

The next day, when it was 1 p.m. and she still hadn't got a call from the number, she tried again and this time the phone was picked up. It was the same voice.

'Yes?'

'Mr Jay Sharma? Sir, this is Divya, Divya Jyothi … You had called yesterday for the interview.'

'Of course, good morning, Miss Divya. How are you?'

'Good morning. I am fine, sir, thank you. I'm calling to confirm that I will be coming to Delhi for the interview.'

'Great, I have all your details, so I will book your tickets and your hotel and send them to you. Okay?'

'Thank you, sir. And sir, I have a request.'

'Sure, please tell me.'

'My mother wants to travel with me. She will pay for her flight, but you need to inform the hotel that there will be two people staying in the room instead of one. I hope this is okay.'

'Of course it is okay. I'll send you the tickets. I look forward to seeing you soon. Best wishes, Miss Divya.'

'Thank you, sir.' The phone was disconnected.

Divya looked at her mother and hugged her.

Two days later, they were at the Hyderabad airport for the flight. Jay had sent the hotel confirmation, and Divya saw online that the hotel was ten kilometres from the airport. The interview was scheduled for the next morning, and their return flight was a few hours after the interview.

Everything was going smoothly, and Divya had every reason to put her guard down. She had the tickets, she had her mother by her side, the company she was going to interview at was legitimate, and the room was booked at a top hotel. But Divya had no clue that her world was about to be turned upside down.

They boarded the plane, and before Divya could switch off her mobile phone, she received a text message from Jay Sharma.

I'll be there at the airport to receive you and your mother, Miss Divya, and drop you to the hotel. See you soon. Jay Sharma.

She looked at her mother and said, 'Jay Sharma, the guy from the company, will be at the airport to receive us.'

Her mother smiled. 'Good.'

'Mom, it is good, but don't you think this is too good? I'm not the company's employee yet, and there is no reason for someone to be so nice to us.'

'Beta, like we are good, he is good too. What's the harm if he picks us up and drops us to the hotel? Sitting at home for the last two months and watching crappy videos on social media has made you so negative. I don't think we need to read too much into this, honey. Everything that happens in the world is not a conspiracy. And I'm right here next to you.'

'You are right, Mom.'

She replied to the message with a 'thank you' and switched off her phone as the plane began to taxi.

Two hours later, they landed at the Delhi airport. The temperature outside, at 11 a.m., was nine degrees. Both took out their jackets and scarves and wore them before getting out.

After collecting their suitcase, as soon as they exited, a man approached them. He was smiling.

'Hi, Miss Divya. I'm Jay Sharma.'

'Hi, sir.'

He turned to Vasundhara and said, 'And this must be your mother.'

Then he bent down and touched Vasundhara's feet. Vasundhara almost jumped back, saying, 'Oh, what you are doing? Please, son.'

Divya said, 'Thank you, Mr Sharma. But you shouldn't have taken the trouble to come personally.'

'I will be truthful—the driver's wife fell sick last night, and I live in Gurgaon, so the airport and the hotel are right on my way to work.'

'Still—I mean, thank you.'

They reached the car park and Jay pressed the remote key to unlock his BMW.

Divya and Vasundhara were shivering due to the walk in the open from the airport's exit to the parking.

The mother and daughter exchanged glances as he placed their suitcase in the boot. Then he opened the door for Divya's mother as Divya opened the door for herself. After this, Jay got into the driver's seat and turned on the ignition.

Switching the heater on, he reached for a thermos and filled two cups with steaming hot soup.

'Here, have some hot soup. It's a cold day and I don't want you people to go back and say Delhi people don't care.'

Divya and her mother took the paper cups, as he continued, 'My wife made this simple tomato and coriander soup. It's vegetarian, as I had no clue if you are vegetarians or non-vegetarians.'

Vasundhara said, 'That's so sweet of her. Yes, we are both vegetarians.'

'Great'. He put the car into gear and pulled it out of the parking lot as Divya and Vasundhara started to drink the soup.

Jay's phone rang. He picked it up and said, 'Hello?'

He listened for a few seconds and said, '*Hun nahin* (Not now).' Then he disconnected.

After a few minutes, to overcome the sudden quietness, Divya said, 'So when is your company planning to open the Hyderabad office?'

'Well, maybe in a month's time. We are looking for properties and also searching for the right people. Setting up a new office has its own challenges, but we are making good progress.'

They finished their soup.

Within minutes, Divya and Vasundhara started to feel drowsy. The last words from Jay they heard were, 'It's all right if you are feeling sleepy. The car is nice and warm now and you are tired. I'll wake you up at the hotel.'

Jay glanced back and smiled. Everything was perfect.

When Divya opened her eyes next, she realized she was on a moving train. She looked around, and Jay's face filled her vision. He had bent down to talk to her.

'What happened? Where are we going? Where is my mother?'

He smiled and said, 'You mother is right here. She is sleeping.'

Divya turned her head and found her mother sleeping on the side berth. But Divya was still feeling lethargic, and her eyes were heavy.

Jay said, 'There is nothing to worry about, Miss Divya. We will soon be at the venue for the interview.'

She said, 'Yes, the interview. How much more time? Can I rest a while?'

'Of course, I will wake you up well before it's time for the interview.'

Divya closed her eyes.

A few hours later, the train pulled into Jhansi railway station. Jay woke Divya and her mother. Both looked around, dazed. But they were too confused to ask anything. Everything seemed hazy and unclear.

Jay helped them get down and carried their suitcase. From the railway station, he hired a taxi and took them to a hotel that was already booked in the name of the mother and daughter. Once in the room, he ordered dinner. By now, it was 9 p.m.

Vasundhara asked Divya, 'How was your interview?'

Divya looked at her. 'Interview? I'm yet to give it.'

Jay said, 'Divya, your interview is already over. You did very well, and the company has offered you the job.'

'Really?' She frowned.

There was a knock on the door. It was room service. Jay took the plates from the man who had brought the food and placed them on the table. Then, with his back towards them, he sprinkled some powder on the food.

Later, as they finished eating, he got up and said, 'Now you please rest. I'll escort you to the airport tomorrow. Good night.'

He left the room. After two hours, using a spare key, he entered the room again and looked around. Divya and Vasundhara were fast asleep.

Jay started with Divya's purse. He found three ATM cards and some cash. Then he turned to Vasundhara's purse and found no ATM cards but some cash. The total cash in both purses was around five thousand. He pocketed the ATM cards but returned the cash to the purses.

After this, he brought his ear close to Divya, turned the voice recorder on his phone on and whispered, 'Miss Divya, you have been successful in the interview. Now we need your bank information to credit your salary.'

She partially opened her eyes and tried to turn her head towards Jay but couldn't.

'To credit your salary, what's the password for your SBI ATM?'

CASE #7: THE BUCK STOPS HERE

'4512,' she whispered.

'Good. Now for Syndicate Bank and ICICI?'

She whispered the codes. Jay smiled and receded. His job was done, and he left the room.

Jay found an SBI ATM and successfully withdrew the cash using all three cards. But due to the limit on daily withdrawals, the total amount didn't add up to even one lakh rupees.

Later that night, he reached his hotel, not far from the one where he had booked Divya and her mother. Then, smiling at the way his mission was progressing, he lay down on the bed and closed his eyes. It was 11 p.m. by then.

The next morning, Jay woke up early. By the time he checked out of the hotel with his small shoulder bag, it was 7 a.m. By 7.15, he was standing in front of Divya and Vasundhara's room.

He knocked on the door and waited. After a minute, he knocked again and placed his ear to the door. There was no sound. Then he took out the spare key from his pocket and opened the door. Inside, the mother and daughter were still asleep.

He called room service and ordered two cups of tea. Then he tried to wake Divya. After some effort, she opened her eyes and looked at him. He was smiling from ear to ear as he helped her sit up in bed, her back against the headboard.

Her lips moved, but before she could say anything, Jay said, 'Miss Divya, I hope you had a great night. Congratulations on your new appointment. How are you feeling today?'

She turned to look at her mother and said, 'What happened to me? Where are we?'

'You are in Delhi, in your hotel. Yesterday evening, you were very tired.'

'My head aches so badly. But I was in a train.'

'Yes, my car broke down, so we travelled a short distance to the hotel by train.'

There was a knock on the door. It was the room service attendant with two cups of tea.

After he left, Jay said, 'Come on now, please have your morning tea. Help me wake your mother up too.'

They tried, but Vasundhara remained asleep. Finally, they gave up, and Jay said, 'We need to fill out a few forms at the bank before we leave for the airport. These forms are required so that your salary can be credited to your account every month.'

'Forms? What forms?' She looked at him, confused.

'Forms that will authorize us to conduct online transfers to your account.'

'I'm feeling very confused. Where do we have to go now?'

'To the bank, Miss Divya.'

'Okay.'

'Do you want this job?'

'Yes.'

'Then please trust me.'

'Yes, I do. But I'm unable to think clearly.'

'Let's go to the bank, and you will feel better once we are there.'

After Divya had her tea, he helped her to her feet and, holding her hand, took her outside the hotel. From there, he hailed an autorickshaw and ordered him to go to the SBI branch.

Within the next half an hour, getting her signature on the withdrawal slip, Jay was able to withdraw ten lakhs in cash from SBI. After that, he took her to an ICICI Bank branch and withdrew another ten lakhs using the same method.

CASE #7: THE BUCK STOPS HERE

With twenty lakhs in his bag, Jay escorted Divya back to her room. By now, Vasundhara had woken up and she was crying, alone and confused.

The moment they entered the room, Vasundhara said, 'Divya, where were you, honey? I have been looking for you.'

Divya hugged her mother and said, 'I was with Jay.'

'Have you got the job?'

'Yes, Mom, I have got the job and the paperwork has been completed too.'

Vasundhara looked at Jay with tears in her eyes and said, 'Thank you, Jay beta.'

Jay didn't know what to say, but he finally managed to mumble, 'Thank you, aunty ji.'

After this, Jay ordered breakfast to the room and sprinkled the same powder on the food before Divya and her mother ate it. After they were unconscious, this time, he removed the gold ornaments from their bodies and left.

The next morning, Divya woke up first. She looked around. Her mother was next to her. She had no idea how much time they had spent in the room. By afternoon, as the effect of the drugs in her body started to wane, she realized for the first time that something fishy was going on. Her mother felt the same way. Divya checked her phone and saw the notifications of cash withdrawals from her bank, as well as the use of her ATM cards. More than twenty lakhs had been withdrawn.

When she looked at herself in the mirror, her hands flew to her neck. Her necklace was missing. So were her bangles, rings and earrings. She checked her mother and found she had no ornaments on her either.

As her head started to clear, she realized that they had been duped.

Divya picked up the phone and called reception. 'What is the name of this hotel?'

'Madam, what? This is Amar Continental.'

'Oh, and what city is your hotel in?'

'What sort of questions are you asking, madam? You are staying in our hotel and want to know what city you're in?'

Divya inhaled deeply. 'Yes, what city am I in?'

'You are in Jhansi, madam.'

The phone dropped from her hand and she sat on the bed heavily.

Vasundhara asked, 'What happened? Are we not in Delhi?'

She looked at her and said, 'We are in Jhansi, Mom.'

'What?'

Divya wondered for a few seconds if she should break the news about the theft or not. Finally, she decided to tell her. There was no way she could handle this crisis alone.

'Mom, that man Jay was a thief. He drugged us and brought us here, and now he has run off with twenty lakh rupees and all our gold.'

'What! Oh my God!' Vasundhara fell onto the bed. She started to say, over and over again, 'Oh my God, oh my God, oh my God …'

'Stop it, Mom. Your God will not come here and return our money. We need to do something.'

CASE #7: THE BUCK STOPS HERE

By 5 p.m., Divya and Vasundhara were standing in front of SHO Bhim Singh at the police station located closest to their hotel.

Bhim Singh listened to them patiently and said, 'Madam, please file an FIR and I assure you that we will do everything we can.'

'Thank you, sir.'

'Can you describe this Jay Sharma in detail?'

'Yes, he was around five feet eight, I think, between twenty-five and thirty, slim and spoke impeccable English. He wore a three-piece suit and was using an iPhone.'

'Body marks? Any accent? Anything peculiar, like colour of eyes, mannerisms …?'

'He looked like a normal corporate manager. He was extremely nice, though—'

'He touched my feet when he met us at the airport,' Vasundhara interrupted her.

The inspector said, 'These are common traits. Anything that would make him stand out?'

'I don't think so.'

'Hmm … do you remember the number of the BMW you travelled in from the airport?'

'I'm sorry but no.'

'Anyway, we will investigate this case on priority. This is the first con of its kind here in Jhansi. I think the criminal chose this place because no one would suspect him here. I'll start with the CCTVs at the banks and the ATMs based on the timings you have mentioned.'

'Will we get our money back, sir?'

'Madam, our team will do everything they can. In all probability, this Jay will be in another city far from here by now. Most probably in some other state, where he will lay low for some time. He is smart, without a doubt. But be rest assured, we will do everything possible to trace him.'

Divya and Vasundhara left Jhansi by a night train in the evening and arrived in New Delhi early the next morning. From Delhi, they took a flight to Hyderabad and were home by afternoon.

For the first few hours, all they did was cry. But as their anger, frustration and helplessness ebbed a bit, Vasundhara said, 'We must file a case in Hyderabad too. After all, we live here.'

Divya looked up and said, 'Right, Mom.'

The next morning, they visited the office of the Hyderabad police in the western zone and complained to the Deputy Commissioner of Police. Their complaint was immediately referred to the detective department. Since it was a case of interstate fraud and the amount involved was substantial, the detective department formed a team.

The team was headed by Inspector Vijay Rao, with ASIs Venugopal Naidu and Mahesh Kumar as the members. Vijay Rao was around forty, fit like a twenty-five-year-old due to his austere habits, and, out of a total experience of fifteen years, he had been with the detective department for the last five years. Word in the department was that if Vijay Rao touched a case, it was most likely to be solved. He was five feet eleven and looked like a film star.

In contrast, Venugopal was a potbellied thirty-five-year-old who looked older than Vijay and was only five feet six inches tall.

He moved slowly and was usually unkempt, but he was known to be good with computers and digital technology—which is why he had been with the detective department for almost a decade.

The third member, Mahesh, was thirty, five-feet-nine and had a pleasing personality, unlike most policemen on the beat, because of which he was a useful hand when it came to interacting with the public. His ticket into the detective department was the fact that people liked to talk to him, divulge secrets and reveal the motivations of others. It was due to these reasons that Mahesh had the maximum number of informers working for him.

In their very first meeting, Vijay looked at Venugopal and Mahesh and said, 'This is a tricky case. Can you guess why?'

Venugopal replied, 'Because the crime took place in another state and the criminal might never have set foot in Telangana.'

'Spot on. And what do you say, Mahesh?'

'Sir, I think gullible people have been cheated by someone who might not be a hardcore criminal. In all likelihood, such criminals leave a trail of breadcrumbs due to a lack of criminal experience.'

'First things first, there is no such thing as a less or more hardcore criminal. A criminal is a criminal. Period. We don't have to take our adversary lightly. Because that's starting on the wrong foot. I know your natural tendency is to trust people, Mahesh, and that's why people trust you too. I don't want to tamper with that quality, but as far as this case is concerned, we are dealing with someone who belongs to another state and has tricked and looted people who live here in Hyderabad. Okay?'

Mahesh nodded and said, 'Yes, of course, sir.'

Vijay continued, 'I think we should leave for Jhansi. That's where we will find our first breadcrumbs.'

Both nodded as Vijay scratched his chin and shared his plan. 'Venu, you stay here in Hyderabad as a backup. We will send information to you from Jhansi, which I want you to run through our tech systems, so that you can parallelly do your own tech-enabled mini-investigation. Mahesh and I will leave tomorrow morning. Are we all on the same page?'

Both nodded, and the meeting was over.

The next morning, Inspector Vijay Rao and Assistant Sub-Inspector Mahesh Kumar boarded a flight for Delhi and covered the rest of the journey, from Delhi to Jhansi, by train, arriving there late in the evening. They were received at the Jhansi railway station by ASI Narkeval, a balding man in his fifties who walked with a slight limp. Narkeval was wearing a leather jacket, and the smell of alcohol was on his breath.

After spending the night at the rest house, Vijay and Mahesh arrived at the SP's office at 9 a.m. the next day. The SP's team had prepared the details, and the SP asked Narkeval to provide the visiting police officers from Hyderabad with all the assistance they needed.

'This way, sir.' Narkeval escorted Vijay and Mahesh to his office at the end of the corridor. Once they settled there, Narkeval said, 'We have gone through the CCTV footage at the banks and the railway station, and we have pictures of our suspect. His name, as per the complaint filed, is Jay Sharma, and here is what he looks like.'

Narkeval tilted the desktop computer towards Vijay and Mahesh and, using the mouse, showed them a total of six images.

CASE #7: THE BUCK STOPS HERE

Vijay said, 'The images are grainy. The one from the railway station may not be reliable because it shows two women and a man walking by the side, and these could be of anyone. But the pictures captured in the ATMs are better.'

Mahesh nodded wordlessly.

Narkeval said, 'Yes, now we know what he looks like. But our preliminary search didn't lead us to anything. We need to dig deeper, of course, which we will.'

Vijay said, 'The suspect looks around thirty to me, which means he must have been on someone's radar, I am sure.'

'Right. Give me your email ID and I'll mail these images to you.'

Mahesh spoke this time. 'Please note it down.'

They were quiet for a few minutes while Narkeval emailed the image files to them. After he had finished, he looked up and said, 'Sent.'

Mahesh checked his mobile phone and, on realizing that he had received it, he said, 'Thank you.'

At that moment, Vijay's phone started to ring. It was Venugopal.

He looked at Narkeval and said, 'I'm sorry, but I need to take this.'

Narkeval nodded. 'Sure, sir.'

Vijay pressed the green icon on his phone and said, 'Yes, Venu?'

'Sir, I have learnt that another woman from Hyderabad was cheated three months ago by a man from Delhi in exactly the same way.'

'Oh! Where was she taken for the interview?'

'To Gwalior.'

'That's in Madhya Pradesh. Whereas Divya and her mother were taken to Jhansi, which is in Uttar Pradesh. Hmm … his crimes have been committed in two different states, whereas he is operating out of Delhi. Venu, have you spoken to this victim in detail?'

'Yes, sir, I spoke to her on the telephone. And she's on the way to our office right now.'

'Keep me posted.'

Vijay disconnected and looked at Narkeval and Mahesh.

Then Vijay said, 'Another woman was duped exactly like this three months ago. We will soon have more details.'

After this, the three of them visited the banks and the hotel where Divya and Vasundhara had stayed, where they presented a picture of the accused, Jay Sharma, and questioned everyone they could.

Although they spent the whole day questioning people, they couldn't get any leads. In the evening, at the rest house, Vijay called Divya and said, 'We are in Jhansi now and we have questioned a lot of people at the banks and the hotel you and your mother stayed in—'

'Have you arrested him?'

Vijay took a deep breath and said, 'We haven't arrested him. Since the crime was committed in Jhansi, he won't be sitting here, will he?'

'Oh yes, sorry. Will we get our money, sir?'

'Look, we are doing what we can. We've come here to pursue all leads. The Telangana police is committed to doing its best. Now, can you tell me more about your conversation with Jay in the car?'

'I have already told you everything, sir.'

'Yes, you have. But maybe you missed something out. I remember you said he lived in Gurgaon and had a wife, the one who made the soup, right?'

'That's what he said. He spoke impeccable English. He had an expensive car. I can't think of anything else. Wait a minute … He got a call while he was driving and he spoke in Punjabi, I think.'

'Can you recall what he said?'

'Hmm … he said, "*Hun nahin.*" Yes, that's what he said. "*Hun nahin.*"'

'That sure is Punjabi. Do you know that another Hyderabad woman was duped like you three months ago?'

'No.'

'Okay, never mind. Thanks, I will get back to you if I need anything else.'

He disconnected and looked at Mahesh.

Mahesh said, 'Yes, sir?'

'Well, there's another state we need to add to the list. Our suspect is Punjabi-speaking.'

The next morning, Vijay received an email from Venu. It was about the arrest of a scamster by the Rajasthan police in Una in Himachal Pradesh. The modus operandi looked similar, and the picture of the accused resembled Jay Sharma, though this man went by the name Sam D'Souza.

Vijay looked at Mahesh after reading it and said, 'Mahesh, someone who looks like Jay Sharma has been arrested by the Rajasthan police. He had scammed a young woman from Bikaner. The MO is similar to our two victims.'

Mahesh stared at the picture of the arrested man. He did look similar to Jay Sharma.

Vijay was soon speaking to Venu. 'Contact the Rajasthan police and try to get as much information as possible about this man.'

'Sure, sir.'

Vijay and Mahesh started to pack to leave Jhansi. Soon, they were on a train to Delhi.

When they were crossing Agra, Vijay's phone rang. It was Venugopal. 'Sir, they have arrested this man in Una in Himachal Pradesh based on a complaint from a woman from Bikaner who was called for a job interview. But the interesting fact is that this woman was not called to Una for the interview.'

'Then where was she called to?'

'To Delhi.'

'This doesn't make sense. If that is the case, how did the Rajasthan police decide to look for him in Una?'

'The victim from Bikaner overheard him telling someone that he would attend a wedding in Una next weekend. She informed the police after she was duped, and they shared the details with the Una police.'

'That makes sense. Mahesh and I will leave for Bikaner from Delhi. You have got four hours to get approval from the DC's office and let us know, okay?'

'Yes, sir.'

Their move was approved, and Vijay and Mahesh took a flight from Delhi to Bikaner.

It was early evening when they landed, and they decided to visit the police headquarters straightaway. From there, they visited the Bikaner jail, where the accused was lodged.

Vijay and Mahesh weren't surprised when they met the accused. He was the man in the pictures they had.

Vijay smiled and said, 'Where is Divya's money?'

He blinked. 'Divya? I don't know any Divya. Look, they have brought me here by mistake.'

'Oh, so you are not the fraudster Jay Sharma?'

He looked straight at them and shook his head. 'Sir, what are you talking about? I'm Sam. That's my name.'

Vijay turned towards Mahesh and nodded. Mahesh pulled out the printouts from the file he was holding and gave them to Vijay.

Vijay started to show Jay the printouts one by one. 'Who is this then?'

Jay didn't reply. Instead, he looked at the floor.

Later, they met the investigating officer (IO) of the Rajasthan police who was handling this case. His name was Bhagwan Kumar.

Inspector Bhagwan Kumar had light eyes but very dark skin. He was around fifty years old, six feet three inches tall and weighed over a hundred kilograms.

After welcoming them into his office, Bhagwan Kumar said, 'So how was the meeting with Sam?'

Vijay replied, 'As far as we are concerned, his name is Jay Sharma. But to answer your question, the meeting was good. Initially, he was evasive, but once we showed him the pictures of him withdrawing money from the banks in Jhansi, he stopped speaking.'

'Well, his real name is Satnam Singh, and he is from Patiala in Punjab. Here, look at his Aadhaar and voter ID card.'

Bhagwan handed over the identification cards of the accused.

Vijay glanced at them and handed them to Mahesh, saying, 'Share these with Venu. He knows what to do next.'

Bhagwan smiled. 'So you want to take him to Hyderabad to face charges?'

'Not right now; we need to dig a little more. Because currently, the charges will not stick.'

'I understand. You do your paperwork and let me know when you want him. We will work out a date with the help of the court. Currently, let him face the music here for what he did to our victim.'

Vijay and Mahesh left the IO's office after that. They spent the entire next day going over the case. Every minute detail was logged in, every piece of evidence, both physical and digital, was recorded and the event diary updated.

Finally, at 7 p.m., Vijay called Venugopal. 'What's up?'

'Good evening, sir, I was about to call you. There has been an interesting development. I coordinated with the Punjab police, and they checked the address mentioned on the suspect's Aadhaar card. The family who stays there says they have never heard of or seen this person.'

'Oh, so this ID is also fake. That means his name is not Jay Sharma, Sam D'Souza or Satnam. Then what the hell is his real name? Venu, please get—'

'Sir, already got approval for your visit to Patiala.'

'Good job.' Vijay disconnected and looked at Mahesh, 'We are going to Patiala.'

Vijay and Mahesh arrived in Patiala the next evening via Delhi and Ambala. They went straight to the address that was mentioned on the suspect's Aadhaar card. The family who lived in the house said they had never seen or heard of Satnam Singh. It was just as expected.

Both of them stepped outside the house and strolled up to a tea stall nearby. It was 8 p.m., and they were shivering due to the bitter cold. They ordered teas.

Vijay asked, 'Mahesh, what do you think we should do next?'

Mahesh replied, 'Sir, he has given this address. I don't think it's arbitrary. This place means something to him. Either he belongs to this city, or he has stayed somewhere here. And our victim Divya also said that he once spoke in Punjabi.'

They sipped the tea in silence, keeping the cups close to their mouths so that the steam warmed their faces. After they finished, Vijay said, 'Let's start asking around. It's like shooting in the dark, I know, but don't forget that we are still shooting and we have a gun.'

Mahesh smiled.

By 9 p.m., they had asked at a few houses and shops. But then the cold intensified and both decided to call it a day.

At 1 p.m. the next day, their luck turned. They were at a shop not more than a kilometre away from the Aadhaar address of the accused, and the shopkeeper recognized Satnam.

The shopkeeper said, 'Sir, this is Gurvinder.'

Vijay smiled and said, 'Gurvinder? Are you sure?'

'Yes, sir. I'm 100 per cent sure.'

'Where does this Gurvinder live?'

Vijay and Mahesh used the shopkeeper's directions and reached a small house another kilometre away. It was locked.

Mahesh knocked at a neighbour's door. A young woman opened the door.

Mahesh smiled and said, 'Madam, I'm sorry, I just want to know when Gurvinder will return.'

From a distance, Vijay saw her smile and reply, 'He has not been in for the last few days. He comes and goes.'

'Who else lives with him in the house?'

'No one. But who are you?'

This was the tricky part of the conversation. Telling the truth was risky, because if this woman was friends with Gurvinder, she would send him a message the minute Vijay and Mahesh left.

'I'm his friend from Delhi. He hasn't been picking up my calls for the last few days, so I was worried. Actually, he owes me money.'

'Owes you money? But ...' She seemed to hesitate. 'How's that possible? He has such a good job and has so much money. He's probably mad at you for something else. It can't be because he doesn't have money to return your loan.'

Mahesh kept his smile in place and asked, 'Would you happen to know what he does for a living?'

'You should know. You're his friend.'

'Well, he told me that he is in the business of providing jobs to people.'

She laughed. 'That's what he told you? He told me that he runs an export-import business.'

Mahesh turned to look at Vijay, who was listening silently.

Vijay smiled, and Mahesh spoke after turning back. 'Will you please tell him that his friend from Delhi was here? My name is Mahesh.'

'Sure, why not?'

'Thank you, madam.'

CASE #7: THE BUCK STOPS HERE

She closed the door.

From there, Vijay and Mahesh went straight to the office of the Superintendent of Police, Patiala. After a detailed discussion and on the basis of the evidence, the SP's office was able to get a search warrant.

The next morning, Vijay and Mahesh, along with two local policemen from the Punjab police, visited the house of the accused. They broke the lock and started to search the small house systematically.

By evening, they had discovered that Gurvinder was the real name of Jay Sharma and that he had created seven identities for himself. They found over thirty lakhs in cash in his house, some jewellery, expensive phones and computers, and designer shoes and clothes. In one of the cupboards, they also found dozens of bottles of expensive imported whisky.

Since Vijay and Mahesh had the record of the serial numbers of the notes withdrawn from SBI and ICICI, they compared it with what they found in the house. Luckily, twelve lakhs of the money belonging to Divya and Vasundhara was unspent. Over the next two days, Vijay and Mahesh recorded the evidence and lifted fingerprints with the help of the forensic department of the Punjab police. It turned out Gurvinder was smart enough not to have committed a single crime in the state of Punjab.

On their return to Hyderabad, the Telangana police filed a case in court. After the hearing, the court directed the present custodian, that is, the Rajasthan police, to produce the accused in Hyderabad. This time, Mahesh and another constable travelled to Bikaner and brought Gurvinder to Hyderabad.

Over the next few weeks, the court heard the arguments, and on the day of the sentencing, Divya and her mother were also present in court. They kept their eyes on him and, after some time, he turned and scanned the room. When his eyes passed over where Divya and her mother were sitting, they didn't stop. Perhaps he didn't even recognize his victims.

Gurvinder was found guilty of the charges and directed to pay the money back to Divya and the other accused. After that, he was sent back to Bikaner jail.

Divya and her mother received the twelve lakh rupees, and the police assured them that, as and when the assets of Gurvinder were liquidated, in accordance with the court's order, the rest of their money would be returned to them too.

A few days later, Divya applied for another job in Hyderabad, and she was accepted.

She returned home and hugged her mother. 'Mom, I have got a job. It's a very large multinational company.'

'That's wonderful news, Divya. Are you happy?'

'Yes, Mom, of course I am happy. This company will pay me 50 per cent more than what I was getting earlier.'

Her mother hugged her again. After a few minutes, as they were drinking coffee, her mother cleared her throat and said, 'Divya, there is a boy …'

A year later, just before announcing the sentence, the judge in Bikaner asked Gurvinder, 'Do you have any last words?'

He nodded, bowed and said, 'Sir, eight years ago, I was tricked by a fraudster who said he would get me a job. He stole two lakhs from me. That was all my family and I had. I went to so many police stations, but no one arrested that person. That's why I decided to become a fraudster myself.'

Gurvinder was sentenced to three years in jail, and his property was confiscated to repay the money he had stolen from various people across the country.

ABOUT THE AUTHOR

Photograph by Darius Chinoy

Kulpreet Yadav is an actor, filmmaker and the author of sixteen books. A product of the Naval Officers' Academy, he spent two decades as an officer in uniform and successfully commanded three ships in his career. Since his retirement as Commandant from the Indian Coast Guard in 2014, he has authored books across diverse genres, including espionage, true crime, war history and romance. With *Dial 100*, Kulpreet delves into the gritty world of true crime, offering readers an insider's perspective on the relentless pursuit of justice.

HarperCollins *Publishers* India

At HarperCollins India, we believe in telling the best stories and finding the widest readership for our books in every format possible. We started publishing in 1992; a great deal has changed since then, but what has remained constant is the passion with which our authors write their books, the love with which readers receive them, and the sheer joy and excitement that we as publishers feel in being a part of the publishing process.

Over the years, we've had the pleasure of publishing some of the finest writing from the subcontinent and around the world, including several award-winning titles and some of the biggest bestsellers in India's publishing history. But nothing has meant more to us than the fact that millions of people have read the books we published, and that somewhere, a book of ours might have made a difference.

As we look to the future, we go back to that one word—a word which has been a driving force for us all these years.

Read.